THE INVISIBLE WOMAN

SHIRLEY ROGERS RADL

THE
INVISIBLE
WOMAN

Target of the Religious New Right

A MERLOYD LAWRENCE BOOK
DELACORTE PRESS/NEW YORK

A Merloyd Lawrence Book
Published by
Delacorte Press
1 Dag Hammarskjold Plaza
New York, New York 10017

Library of Congress Cataloging in Publication Data
Radl, Shirley Rogers.
The invisible woman.
"A Merloyd Lawrence book."
Bibliography.
Includes index.
1. Housewives—United States. 2. Women—Employment—
Social aspects—United States. 3. Sex discrimination—United States.
4. Moral Majority, Inc. 5. Conservatism—United States.
6. Christianity and politics. 7. Fundamentalism.
I. Title.
HQ1426.R33   1983   305.4′2′0973
ISBN 0-385-29232-5
ISBN 0-385-29210-4 (pbk.)
Library of Congress Catalog Card Number 83-5345

TABLE OF CONTENTS

	ACKNOWLEDGMENTS	xi
I	THE NEW WAR ON WOMEN	1
II	WHOSE BODY IS IT, ANYWAY?	31
III	THE BOTTOM LINE	54
IV	WEEP FOR THE CHILDREN	69
V	WOMAN AGAINST WOMAN, WOMAN AGAINST HERSELF	90
VI	SEX, DRUGS, ROCK AND ROLL— NOW IT'S TIME FOR MIND CONTROL	121
VII	IT CAN NEVER HAPPEN IN AMERICA	148
VIII	WITH THE BRAINS GOD GAVE YOU . . .	164
	BIBLIOGRAPHY	183
	INDEX	189

To the memory of my parents,
whose devoted example taught me
that the preservation of the family
rests largely on a four-letter word—
love.

So it is with gratitude and love
that I dedicate this book
to my mother and my father,
who truly must be in heaven:

Henrietta Joyce Kenna Rogers
November 4, 1904, to January 20, 1973

Robert Chancy Rogers
May 30, 1903, to January 27, 1973

ACKNOWLEDGMENTS

Merloyd Lawrence is an editor who really knows how to reject a manuscript. She doesn't simply return it with a letter saying, ". . . does not suit our editorial needs . . ." but instead may, as she did with mine, write a few lines that can inspire an author to look at a current work from an entirely new angle. In this instance what I had intended as the core of a book became instead one chapter—and a launching-off place for a book I never thought I could write.

And however inspired, I probably couldn't have written the book were it not for the unflinching support of a number of dear friends. At about the same time that Merloyd sowed the seeds for this book, my friend Penny Gerbode, whom I'd been out of touch with for over five years, came back into my life. Her enthusiasm for my written words and her absolute faith in my ability to communicate what she saw so clearly as a threat to women inspired in me the confidence I needed to perform an immense task in a very limited amount of time. Penny gave me a sense of myself as a writer and an agitator when I needed it the most. That she never wavered in her support gave me the strength I needed to see it all the way through.

And then Marjorie Klemp, a new and very dear friend to whom I was drawn because of our mutual concerns over the plight of women, not only offered similar support but, without my ever asking, combed the library for much of the material I needed for a crash course on the far right. Along with her friendship and support, she also gave me the benefit of all of her knowledge of history and religion, critiqued material, made suggestions, and served as my sounding board.

And I found a new and extraordinary friend, Cheryl Landers, in the workaday world. The support and actual help she gave me over these many months made all the difference between this book making it on schedule and, I sometimes think, not making it at all. "What can I do to help?" she would ask while reminding me when I dawdled to keep my priorities in order. "Your first priority is the book," she would say. I am so grateful to her for helping me to keep that rule.

A very special note of thanks must go to my agent, Kathy Robbins, for her devotion to this project, her sound advice, and the sympathetic ear when needed. But mostly I want to thank her for giving me a new lease on my career—and hence, on my life.

And for helping to protect that career by protecting me against myself, I would be remiss not to acknowledge and thank attorney Dick Malina.

Finally, coming full circle, I'm enormously indebted to Merloyd Lawrence for being such an outstanding editor. Merloyd asked the right questions, kept me on course when I would start to stray, and cheered me on all the way. Her commitment to this book has been as complete as my own.

THE INVISIBLE WOMAN

I

THE NEW WAR ON WOMEN

The more I work with the issue of the ERA, the more I realize that the women's liberation movement is antifamily. . . .
They are for the Equal Rights Amendment, which would take away the marvelous legal rights of a woman to be a full-time wife and mother in the home. . . .

Phyllis Schlafly
as quoted in *Listen America!*
by Jerry Falwell, 1981

Equality of rights under the law shall not be denied or abridged by the United States or by any state on account of sex.

A proposed constitutional
amendment

You haven't come a long way, and you're not a baby.

Message on a T-shirt

A Question of Place

For some of us the idea that "a woman's place is in the home" became both academic and anachronistic in light of financial circumstances that compelled us to work. For others it became anachronistic with the realization that women are born with no less talent or intelligence than males and, unless it is conditioned out of us, no less of a desire to be independent and make our way in the world.

Over the past decade or so the media have heralded great strides for women, depicting them as they enter professions traditionally open only to men. Women are delaying motherhood to establish themselves in careers, forgoing motherhood altogether, or, seemingly, grabbing the whole pie—husbands, children, and careers. We hear of such paragons as Sandra and Daryl Bem, both Stanford University professors who have worked out the egalitarian dream, or Leona Egeland, a wife and mother who successfully ran for a seat in the California Assembly a number of years back. We read of mothers who are doctors, lawyers, biochemists, physicists, telephone linepersons, technical managers, company vice-presidents, public relations specialists, editors, publishers, literary agents, TV anchors, photojournalists, you name it. Our local newspaper, *The Peninsula Times Tribune*, summed it all up in an eight-page spread, "The Changing Role of Women in the 80's." This featured a woman county supervisor, a former ambassador to the United Nations, an assistant public defender, a home builder, a management consultant, a woman returning to school for her doctorate, and even a female astronaut. Laced in between were trendy and inspiring pieces on everything from quality child care to quality time with children, with stress, time, and financial management completing the picture. What made this feature so significant to me is that Palo Alto is or was the last bastion of traditional supermotherhood. That feminism had finally overwhelmed this community made me realize that the notions of woman's place that I grew up with had finally been put to rest.

However, over the picture painted by the articles on mass liberation another picture, with increasingly broader strokes, is being superimposed. This is becoming apparent from articles about women who delayed parenthood to establish themselves in careers and then, surprisingly, decided that their place, once they had children, was at home, because that's what was right for them. A less benign form of this view is becoming more generalized. An ominous example is an article in the March 1982 issue of the *Ladies' Home Journal* reviewing the growing animosity between housewives and career women. Written by Nancy Rubin, the article dramatizes what the author calls "the new cold war between housewives and working mothers."

Unlike a number of women I know or have read about who have chosen to stay home but who consider such decisions determined by their circumstances and, less frequently, personal preference, the housewives in the *Journal* article are very quick to say that they feel that *all* mothers should stay home. They lob heavy criticism at career women who have children and then run back to their jobs, while they, the housewives, defend their choice to stay home to "raise decent kids," implying that working mothers *don't* raise decent kids. The career women who were interviewed, on the other hand, had a few nasty words for the housewives, who, as a group, are seen as smug and judgmental or even hopeless neurotics.

What disturbed me just as much as the hostility expressed by these women and the fact that this debate was being aired in a national magazine was that the article focused only on housewives and career women, supporting what I now know to be a widespread myth: American mothers are graced with the full freedom to determine what they will do with their lives and are thus divided into two distinct camps: career women who work for fulfillment and housewives who are financially well off enough to be able to stay home.

This myth ignores the facts: Homemakers currently represent only one seventh of all American women, and only two percent of all people—men and women alike—work in fulfilling jobs and do so out of choice. Ask a mother who works in an ordinary job one question: "If you inherited a million dollars, would you continue in your present job?" Ask it not only of women, but also of men, and you will conclude, as I have, that most people work because they need the money. Increasing numbers of women who are already mothers, with children under the age of six, are joining the ranks of those of us who know that those "marvelous legal rights" to stay home that Phyllis Schlafly fusses about are a figment of that lady's imagination or the invention of her script writer.

But that fact goes largely ignored because a strange marriage has been made between the popular press and the Religious New Right. In one corner are the progressive journalists who, for the past decade or so, have shone the spotlight on career women, sending the message to all women that they can follow their own star. From the beginning they have put across the idea of *choice*. And now that they have started to pay attention to the woman who is a housewife out of choice, the myth of choice is a stronger one. And this myth gives grist to the media's dubious partner in the other corner, the New Right leaders who blame highly visible career women for the decline of the American family. Pointing to our national 40 percent di-

vorce rate, teenage sexual activity, and drug abuse, their case goes
like this: The women's movement has created such unhappiness in
housewives and such a need for women to fulfill themselves that they
turn their backs on their femininity and their family responsibilities,
neglect their children, leave their husbands, and go off and "do their
own thing"; and this is why, in a nutshell, our divorce rate is so high
and the morality of our young people, deprived of traditional home
environments, is so low.

This argument is but one of many simplistic explanations of complicated social and human issues that the New Right puts out; because it is so simply and so constantly stated, whether true or not, it
has become widely believed.

There now exists an army of millions of foot soldiers who perpetuate this myth of choice as it is stated by the New Right leadership.
These soldiers are members of Fundamentalist Baptist churches,
ultraconservative Catholic church groups, and the very large and
powerful Mormon Church. The more visible generals they follow,
and hence the ones I will focus on, are Phyllis Schlafly, head of the
Eagle Forum and Stop ERA; the Reverend Jerry Falwell, star of *The
Old Time Gospel Hour,* pastor of the Thomas Road Church in
Lynchburg, Virginia, and President of the Moral Majority, Inc.;
Spencer Kimball, President of the Mormon Church; Ezra Taft Benson, member of the Council of Twelve and heir-apparent to the presidency of the Mormon Church; and Pat Robertson of the Christian
Broadcast Network, host of *The 700 Club,* a religious talk show, and,
more recently, the brains behind a soap opera that peddles tradition,
religion, and morality. There is an assortment of electronic preachers,
religious-political leaders, legislators, politicians, and other groups
such as the National Right-to-Life Committee. They have named
themselves "The New Right"; they say they are politically conservative. But mainline political conservatives disavow this latter claim
and say instead that this coalition is a radical movement, not a conservative Republican one.

Whatever the labels, the influence of this movement can be seen in
the way it has managed to resurrect the argument about "woman's
place" and make the myth of choice—that women are either careerist
or housewives because they have those options—a pervasive one.

The existence of this myth has resulted in making the one woman
who is representative of the majority of us *invisible.* This is the

woman who works out of economic necessity—through no choice of her own. Her seeming nonexistence in the eyes both of the righteous right-wing and of the media who have spotlighted women with dazzling careers has had the net effect of diminishing her as a person and trivializing not only her plight, but the monumental job she does in combining work with the care of her family. *She* is mainstream America, but she doesn't exist.

Despite the claims of the media and the New Right, she has not come a long way. An ironic case in point is that of a woman who wrote to me:

> Ten years ago, after my first baby was born, I wanted to return to my old job. But my husband said he wouldn't permit it—that I was a mother and my place was at home with the baby. I didn't fight him, and then three years later we had another child, and by then I'd settled into being a housewife. I really got into it—taking care of the kids, cooking, sewing, and the whole homemaking thing.
>
> And then one night not long ago over dinner, my husband told me, "Well, we just can't make ends meet. Looks like you'll have to get a job."

What separates this woman from most mainstreamers I know is that she had *wanted* to return to work, and the reason she had wanted to was that she had had a career as a publicist that she enjoyed. That she has by no means come a long way is evidenced by the fact that her husband called the shots on both occasions when the question of her working came up. What gives his about-face a sad and ironic twist is that where once she could have returned to a job she found rewarding, the years out of circulation meant that her contacts and her public-relations skills had eroded. As it turned out the only marketable skills she had retained were clerical ones. Where once she would have been happy to go to work, this predicament was cause for depression.

And she is just one of the growing number of women who have been forced to return to work. Representative of the many women I've talked to is Jan, who told me:

> When it became apparent that I had to go back to work, my children were small, and I felt they needed me. At the time I

was very involved in their lives, participating in the cooperative nursery school and doing other things for them simply beyond taking care of them. I cooked and sewed, and I had the most beautiful garden imaginable. I remember feeling a bit of resentment that what I was doing didn't seem to be valued by my friends who were always talking about their jobs. I resented what I felt were the subtle pressures of the feminist movement to get a "real" job.

But when all was said and done, it was not the pressures from women's lib that sent me back to work in an office. I was very fulfilled in my role as a homemaker and had no desire to work in an office, so it was not because of any external or internal pressure that I went back. The cost of living is what sent me to work.

Brushing that truth aside, Jerry Falwell offers his own interpretation of the financial need that propels us out of our homes. In his book *Listen America!* (1981) he tells us:

Many women today say they must work for economic reasons. Although inflation has placed a financial burden on the family, we are overly concerned about materialistic wealth. Many Americans consider it more important to have several cars in the driveway, a beautiful house, and two color television sets than have a stable home environment for their children.

Really? Several cars in the driveway? How many people do you know who have several cars in the driveway? Not only do I not know anyone who has, I do not know one working mother who is working to add another motor vehicle to the family fleet. And the only people I know personally who are buying their own homes are either those who broke into the housing market before real-estate prices and soaring interest rates made it impossible to do so or those who have lots of money. For most young couples today, home ownership is but an elusive dream. Speaking to this point, Lisa, who works as a secretary and would prefer not to work at all, told me:

When I got married I had this picture of what life would be like. We would have two children, and I'd stay home with them. Home would be a nice little three-bedroom house somewhere in the suburbs. Well, we have the two children, but nice little three-bedroom houses in the Bay Area start at about $175,000, and those are usually advertised under the heading, "Handyman Special," which means that they're about to slide off their foundations. Not only would it be impossible to save enough for the down payment on one of those wrecks, but my income was essential to our being able to afford the first and last months rent on our apartment, the rent of which is just about equal to my take-home pay for one month.

I very much resent it that I have to work, and I very much resent that attitudes haven't changed very much. There are still people who disapprove of a working mother. Other mothers who don't have to work, schoolteachers, and even near strangers have criticized me for this.

Already feeling guilty for leaving her children to go back to work, when she is criticized by those who believe she has a choice in the matter, she feels even guiltier. While a few years back the guilt working mothers felt may not have actually subsided, at least there existed a brief period where it wasn't often tapped into by others and brought painfully to the surface. But in the last two or three years I've noticed a revival of the disapproval that makes it very difficult for a mother to defend working. While this is a real problem for women in general, it must be much more so for those who are members of churches whose leaders equate a mother's working with gross sinfulness. As one lovely Christian woman told me:

I work because we need the money to maintain a decent lifestyle. I'd rather be home because it would be easier. And I feel so guilty leaving my daughter. But one of the reasons we need some of the money I earn is that we send our daughter to church school, something we're told we must do. But my working has caused friends in the church to treat me differently—with disapproval. And whenever our pastor talks about men's and women's roles, I feel he's speaking directly to me. The result is guilt on guilt.

In the January 1982 issue of *McCall's Working Mother* there appeared an article, "Thou Shalt Not Work," written by Christine Rigby Arrington. The author, herself a Mormon, interviewed a number of devout church women who must suffer their church's condemnation of working women. "As economic necessity collides with the tenets of their church," she writes, "many working mothers feel tortured both by their own guilt and by others' hostile criticism."

The tactics employed by church leaders to instill this punishing guilt and to push women back into their homes (whether or not they, in fact, can afford to go home again) begins with callously dismissing actual financial need, as Jerry Falwell does, while chastising women for being too materialistic. It apparently works. As one woman told me, "I feel guilty every time I buy a blouse I need to wear to work. I see that not as a need, though my closet is sparse, but as evidence of my own materialism." Another tactic is to imply that the husbands of working women are "bad providers." Ezra Taft Benson, for example, enjoys keeping alive the myth that a woman's working robs a husband of his masculinity. Naturally the leaders push all of the maternal buttons we all have when they invoke Proverbs 29:15: "The rod and reproof give wisdom: but a child left to himself bringeth his mother to shame."

A reflexive response of those church women who may already feel guilty for going against their churches' rules by working is simply to parrot the scripture without paying attention to what it really says and how it may apply to them. Since when is leaving a child in the care of someone else the same as leaving a child alone? The scripture says nothing at all about a woman staying home and nothing at all about a mother temporarily leaving a child with another responsible adult—least of all at a day-care center or nursery school. Does this scripture apply to a woman who must leave her child in the care of another to go into the hospital? But those who spout scripture to make their points are not interested in modern applications, or such fine points of interpretation as the fact that the scripture speaks only of leaving a child *alone*.

This is a catch-22 for the woman who doesn't want to work, but is forced to. For making what she considers to be a supreme sacrifice, she's criticized not just by the leaders of her church but by the very people she'd trade places with in a minute—righteous housewives who can afford to stay home. When a woman returns to the executive suite or to the classroom in pursuit of a degree, she may have her detractors, but she also has a cheering section among her approving liberated sisters. Few, however, thanks to all of the emphasis on superwomen, will ever applaud a woman who goes to work as a secretary because she needs the money.

Another catch-22 of the ninth decade of the twentieth century is expressed by the reluctant working mother who told me, "When I got pregnant, I planned to stay home and take care of my own baby. But just the fact of this child's existence is what makes it necessary for me to work."

When the media focus on women who work for fulfillment, not only is the woman who might prefer not to work at all ignored, but those who truly hate their jobs have escaped notice altogether. Their abject misery may not be as great as that of those who dwell at poverty's door, but it is very real.

Claire, an executive secretary, told me, "I would give anything in the world just to walk straight out the door." She said that when she knew she'd have to get a job, she told herself it might be exciting to get out in the world: "You know, get dressed up every day, have my hair done, be with people, be part of something."

Claire's "exciting" day begins with her making coffee and washing any dishes that are lying around—at the office, after she has performed identical tasks at home. Once the coffee is perking and the dishes are washed, Claire then moves on to straighten up her boss's office. "He scatters newspapers, reports, and files all over the place, and part of my job is to keep him organized." The scene sounds like a messy adolescent's bedroom: "One day I even found a necktie and a sock on the floor mixed in with all the debris."

I place his telephone calls for him, I shop for him, I get his coffee and his snacks for him. I take lunch orders for everyone in the office and then go to the deli to pick everything up. I type, I file, and run and fetch. He has me running and fetching for him all day, and it wears me out. It's just a big power trip with him. It's his way of putting me in my place—his way of reminding me that I'm an underling.

I cannot tell you how much I hate this job. I stay because the last one was just as bad, and if I keep jumping from job to job, that will give me a record of instability.

Cheryl, who works in a bank, misses her baby while she's at work and dislikes her job so much that she cries every night on her way home from work.

The work is shit, and the environment is even worse. I stayed home after my first child, who is now eight, was born, and I had every intention of staying home with this much-wanted baby. But the point is, when I went back to work after having stayed home for eight years, I couldn't believe what I found. I was a thirty-five-year-old "girl," who had to be told to be on time and be told to do the work. My God, here I've been raising a child, and suddenly I found I was being treated like one. It was somehow assumed that if I wasn't supervised, I'd try to get away with something.

The men, on the other hand, go out for three-martini lunches, and that is okay because it is considered to be business—even when they take along their girl friends. They can run personal errands during working hours because, I'm told, rank has its privileges. But when I ask for time off to take a child to the doctor or the dentist, my boss behaves as if I'd asked for an all-expenses-paid trip to Las Vegas. The women at our bank have to *justify* any deviation from the routine, but the men do not.

Times may have changed, but in some offices, apparently, women are still treated differently from men. We are abundantly aware that they do not receive comparable pay for comparable work, but it isn't always apparent to those who do not work in ordinary jobs that women are still treated like children, mental defectives, or inferior creatures.

Or worse. The experiences of Patricia, who went to work in a construction job after the city of Palo Alto opened it up for women, were not those touted by progressive media:

I had these big dreams. I was going to break the barrier. I'd been reading about how more and more women were doing men's jobs. I felt superior to other women who settled for secretarial and clerical jobs, and I was going to strike a blow for equality, so I joined the construction gang.

Well, I broke a barrier all right, and then the barrier broke me. It was eight hours of derision every day. I was constantly needled by the men for not being able to do things as well as they could—although they were experienced and I was still learning. I was accused of being a "dyke," and asked about my "queer relationships." If I read a book at lunchtime—which I did because no one would eat with me—I was later asked what sort of porno I read—how big the guy's dick was, and so forth. I am, by the way, not a lesbian, and I do not read pornography. I would like to know where these brownshirts got the idea that because I'm a feminist, those things necessarily follow.

Needless to say, I was never "one of the crew." I was so *lonely,* and I could feel the total lack of respect—the contempt, actually, the men held for me. Here I was, a single mother who had to work to support two children, and I was treated like a piece of shit every hour of every day.

Don't ever let anyone tell you that it's easy, glamorous, or exciting to try to do that kind of work—or that any woman really can step out of the stereotypical role. I could do the work, all right, but I never expected to be so abused. Nobody ever told me—all I ever heard was that things had changed and women could make it in such jobs.

A remark I heard a railroad worker make with respect to how affirmative action was working in his company underscores Patricia's view—and mine—that the options that women have now have been greatly exaggerated by both the liberal press and the New Right. "Now they want separate toilet facilities. I say that if they want to do men's work, they can use the urinals just like everyone else."

When it comes to employment, a woman's place is generally still with other women. Reporting on recent studies in *The Peninsula Times Tribune* (August 27, 1982), Mary Ann Seawell writes:

> "Most establishments are about as segregated as they can be," according to William T. Bielby, associate professor of sociology at the University of California at Santa Barbara, and James T. Baron, who is moving from UC–Santa Barbara to become assistant professor of organizational behavior at the Stanford University Graduate School of Business. . . .
>
> Segregation means fewer training opportunities, advancement possibilities, and less salary potential for women. "We repeatedly encountered instances where sex segregation meant successively greater authority and responsibilities for men and 'dead-end' employment for women," Bielby and Baron said.

Baron could think of no instance in which women make up ten percent of a job field but fill most or all of the supervisory posts in that field.

Walk through any elementary school and you will find that most of the teachers there are women, but the principal is nearly always male. All of the hype to the contrary, there still exists to a very large extent Man's Work and Woman's Place.

The Invisible Girls

In the spring of 1980 I learned first-hand about options. When, for a number of reasons, the completion of a book I'd been working on for two years was put off, delaying the second half of the advance, the first thing I learned was that I no longer had the "marvelous right" to continue living as I'd been living for the past nine years—as a wife and mother in the home and a free-lance writer.

It was with no small amount of dread that I set out to exchange my life at home during the day for one in an office. However, I did strive for a positive attitude when I went to the employment agency. And there I learned what my options were: having published four books and over thirty articles in national magazines, having established and administered a parental-stress hot line, having nine years earlier served as executive director of a national environmental organization, having done much community service work, and having run a home added up to "no experience." Thus, I had but one option, owing solely to the fact that I nearly knocked the eyes out of my counselor with my rapid-fire typing skills—acquired in the course of writing professionally. The option: entry-level secretary. This was confirmed at all of my interviews, where I further learned that I could begin as a secretary to remain one forever.

Too many serendipitous things have occurred in my life for me not to have a sense of destiny. Looking back, I now realize that destiny sent me to this particular office, one of a number in which I worked, where I was called a "girl" six times before nine o'clock, was told to make a pot of coffee, and then answered the phone to hear a male voice at the other end of the line inquire, "Is anybody there?"

It was on this same day that my new boss called me into his office to introduce me to a business executive. "Shirley, this here is Bill," he said. "Bill, this here is Shirley, and she'll be working closely with me, so I want you to get to know each other." And then he curled his lip into something that was trying hard to be a smile and said, "Bill here would probably like a cup of coffee, babe." When I asked Bill Here how he liked his coffee, Bill said, "Hot and black. Just like my women, honey."

The next day, when Bill came in, I was sitting at the front desk filling in for the receptionist. As he sat down on the sofa to await his audience with my boss, he picked up *The Wall Street Journal,* opened up the paper, looked through me, and said, simply, "Black," and commenced reading. And without looking up when I came back with his coffee, he said, "Thank you, Sylvia."

This was an office through which dozens and dozens of people in the money business passed each day, and it took no time at all to learn that in this environment the men were men and the women were girls—two distinct classes of citizens. There existed not one iota of equality, for a person's worth was based on gender, how much money you dealt with, what sort of car you drove, how much power you had, and your capacity to screw others at the bargaining table. I came away from that experience with a deeply held conviction that the financial world is the last bastion of the superswine—the one that many of us had thought had disappeared from the American landscape. You know the one—the brownshirt in the Brooks Brothers suit who never sees his wife and kids at night, thinks racial jokes are as funny as lewd ones, and has a girl friend half his age.

Officially my duties consisted of general secretarial work and managing the office. However, I spent half my time paying my boss's personal bills, straightening out his accounts at department stores, spot-cleaning his jacket, having flowers sent wherever, and getting his car gassed up at the service station he had to pass on his way to the office. When I performed these tasks competently, I was rewarded with praise: "Good girl."

When, on occasion, my boss dictated to me, the ritual went something like this: I would sit and he would stand, of course, clearly establishing his power base. He would pace back and forth, look up at the ceiling, knead his crotch, and start by dictating the name and address from the letterhead just before handing it to me. He would walk behind me and place his hands on my shoulders and give them a little squeeze. There would be a routine invitation to go to his house and sit naked with him in his Jacuzzi, and then I would suggest that we get on with the dictation. He would then dictate a few words, move around so that he was facing me, give his crotch another pull, and belch. This rumbling belch lasted for several seconds. Being well brought up, I never reacted, which seemed to call for more drastic action: He would fart once, and then dictate right on to the end.

As I was not expert at it, it was the receptionist's job to massage the knots of battle out of his neck while I tended to the task of getting him his orange juice and snacks.

Once he told us, "No wife of mine will ever work. A woman should stay home where she belongs and take care of her husband and children."

A pearl, I think, for the times; for coming out of the mouth of a man five years my junior who possessed two advanced degrees, and for being courageously stated in 1980. Here are a few other pearls cast before us by the swine:

"It's a well-known fact—it's been documented, you know—that women who have big boobs have small brains.

"Women are emotionally unstable. Everyone knows that. It's because they have menstrual periods.

"You want equal rights?" he once told a room full of working women. "Then learn to support yourselves."

I want to emphasize that I worked in this office in the early eighties. *Nineteen* eighties. The office had everything—everything needed to drive an existent reality home to a sheltered feminist who had happily and naively believed that overt sexism had gone the way of the myth about certain covert activity causing blindness or hair growth on the palms of the hands. Although I actually managed the office, for example, a man whose total working experience had consisted of having been a used-car salesman held the title "Office Manager." And, oh, how he managed: He would stand in the middle of the large room where the bookkeepers and I worked and appear to oversee—not unlike a job foreman in a factory. When he wasn't standing, he would move from one "work station" to the next, peering over our shoulders and occasionally inquiring, "Is that company business you're working on?" He also took three-hour lunches and conducted all of his personal business at the office, though he chastised the "girls" for taking an occasional personal phone call. Phone calls. His were placed by anyone who was female and happened to be handy. For this he was paid considerably more than the females who did the actual work. That he always wore a cowboy hat was a nice touch.

There was, of course, more. Much more. But I think you get the picture. As I can almost hear the question being asked, I will attempt an honest, if confused, answer. I stayed for as long as I did simply because I had no reason to believe that any secretarial job—which was all I was led to understand I could hope for—would be any better. Why leave the frying pan for a possible fire? Why start over somewhere else only to find that it might even be worse? And so I stayed until I could afford to act on my choice not to.

Although I had possessed serious doubts that it would ever happen, the delayed book was completed, and soon afterward a most gratefully received check was in my mailbox. Fortified, I followed our poor beleaguered receptionist's lead and tendered my resignation. These "blatant acts of disloyalty" brought out one last pearl from our former employer: "The cause of all this trouble here—you and her leaving and all—is that some people think they can think for themselves. And some people actually think they have the right to make their own decisions and run their own lives."

Could there be a shadow of a doubt in anyone's mind that, compared to working in that office, staying at home would have been absolute paradise?

While it requires a certain suspension of disbelief to accept this description of my experience—what I went through myself nearly every day—it is an honest account. Other experiences, though not quite as extreme, have contributed to my conviction that, of all office positions, the one that holds the greatest potential—by virtue of its running and fetching functions—to demean a woman most is that of secretary. Since leaving that truly terrible job and working in other places, I have seen nothing to persuade me otherwise. With all due respect to secretaries themselves, frequently they are perceived by some who employ them as objects—things. In some cases they are status symbols, and while having one is an indicator of status, having a well-behaved one is even better: "My girl really toes the mark."

Another woman who also happens to be a professional writer has put her toes into the secretarial pool. In the "My Turn" column of *Newsweek,* October 4, 1982, Karen Kenyon tells of a similarly depressing experience, and then makes this observation about the secretarial role:

> We think we have freed our slaves, but we have not. We just call them by a different name. Every time people reach a certain status in life they seem to take pride in the fact that they now have a secretary.
>
> It is a fact that it has to be written very carefully into a job description just what a secretary's duties are, or she will be told to clean off the desk, pick up cleaning and the like. Women in these jobs are often seen as surrogate wives, mothers and servants—even to other women.

Even very special and prestigious "secretarial" positions, if they are held by females, can be rather demeaning. For example, a few months after a good friend of mine very gleefully accepted an appointment as press secretary to the governor of a very large state, she called and told me, "Shirl, a secretary is a secretary is a secretary." In her $45,000-per-year job (the males occupying the same grade-level positions earned $47,000), she explained that she knew she had arrived, that she was truly one of the inner circle, a member of the trusted staff, the day she got to pack his bag for a trip and then carry it and his briefcase as they boarded the plane.

So much for working for fulfillment.

The Egalitarian Fantasy

Not only does all of the current idiotic debate over careers versus homemaking keep the majority of working mothers invisible, it also obscures one of the most obvious and compelling reasons many mothers would prefer not to work outside the home.

Typically, the ordinary working woman, a member of the invisible majority we rarely hear about, does not have the egalitarian marriage career women are supposed to have. For that matter, most career women probably don't have such a thing either. According to Laraine T. Zappert, a clinical psychologist at Stanford University, "women set extremely high standards for themselves" when it comes to homemaking. They feel, she said, in a paper presented to the American Psychological Association in Montreal, that they must do more than men and be the best in all they do. "All" includes child care and household tasks, for which women still assume primary responsibility. Regardless of career status, Zappert found, even when both husband and wife are employed outside the home, the traditional division of labor still exists. Women who have combined a career and domesticity, she says, have often internalized society's dictum: "It's okay if you go to work as long as you don't give up the other stuff."

As difficult as this is for the career woman, it is more so when *he* has the career, and she simply has a job. When her major responsibilities are that of being a wife and mother, often she is more self-conscious about how she performs in that role. Add to that the belief that her work is trivial as compared to his and you have a complete blueprint for unfairness. As one woman told me, "Since his job is more important than mine, he's more tired than I, and that means that I have to do all the housework." Another said that her husband eagerly accepted the paycheck she brought home, but saw her working as some sort of a "hobby" and insisted that she always bear in mind that her major responsibilities were taking care of him and the children, and she thus needed to keep "her priorities in order." Still another woman told me that when she tried to get her husband to help more, he told her flatly, "The day you bring home as much money as I do is the day we'll talk about an equal division of the housework."

Zappert's study comes as no surprise. It is not the only one to demonstrate that the egalitarian dream is an elusive one for most working mothers. In May of 1978 *Redbook* sponsored a survey, the results of which revealed that a majority of American husbands of working women share the housework little or not at all, while a scant twelve percent share equally. Then, in April of 1980, *McCall's Working Mother* published a report saying that although more mothers than ever are now working, they get less help than ever from their husbands. Summing up the report findings, sociologist Richard Berk declared, "Husbands do zilch."

What scholars call "anecdotal" research provides the details that statistics and studies do not. Lisa, who starts her day at 5:30, exemplifies the plight of the working mother of small children. She gets the baby ready nearly before her eyes are open, helps her four-year-old get dressed, gives both of them breakfast, gets dressed herself, makes a pass at clearing away the breakfast dishes so she doesn't have to come home to them, and then tucks everyone into the car. Then she moves out into traffic and gets onto the freeway, where she joins the convoy of working moms driving their kids to child care. She arrives at the sitter's in a deranged state, she says, from being in bumper-to-bumper traffic with one child wailing his lungs out and the four-year-old kicking out an accompaniment on the back of her seat. After a ritual discussion with her sitter about constipation and pinworms, Lisa gets back into traffic and is lucky if she arrives at the office by nine o'clock.

It is after five, after she has put in a full day and then repeats, in reverse, the traveling arrangements, that Lisa assumes her role as a housewife. Once she gets home, she makes dinner, feeds the baby, gets him ready for the night, and eats her own supper on the run. Before she goes to bed, she does a little laundry, does a little housework, packs the diaper bag, makes snacks for the children for the next day, and gets the coffee set up to brew at a flick of the switch in the morning. She says that her entire life is consumed with work.

I have no time. No time for love, for laughter, for enjoying the children I adore. All I have time for is maintenance and yelling at my four-year-old when he makes a mess I'll have to clean up. I don't watch television, I don't read, I have no hobbies, and my husband and I never go anyplace. Now that I think about it, the only friends I have are the women I work with. I have no social life, but then I don't want one—I used to, but now I'd rather have time to do nothing at all. Or sleep.

Lisa takes caffeine tablets to keep going. "I would nod off at my desk if I didn't because I have to get up with the baby at night."

Another woman told me that she is convinced, as evidenced by the fact that he reads the newspaper while she runs around, that her husband has absolutely no idea of all there is to do. While he does a few small things, she says, he behaves as if family meals on the table and a clean house are givens, no more difficult to achieve than turning on a switch when one needs electrical power.

One night I told him he'd just have to help more, and he looked at me like I was crazy and said, "Look, what's the big deal? I got you a microwave, a washer, a dryer, a dishwasher, a

garbage compactor. All you have to do is push a few buttons."
I'm at a loss as to how to explain to him, without it seeming like
I'm whining, that there's a lot more to housework than pushing
a few buttons.

Other invisible chores that women do—what Ivan Illich has called
"shadow work"—include driving the children to and from the sitter's
(giving them less time at home than their husbands), taking children
to the doctor, dentist, orthodontist, the skin specialist, and shopping
for clothes. Virtually every one of the dozens of women I talked to
said that they assumed responsibility for all of these tasks and more:
taking pets to the vet, going with teenagers to traffic court, driving
children to various activities, helping with homework. Claire explained it this way:

> Everything that relates to the kids is my responsibility. My
> husband has never even met our pediatrician. And most of the
> time I go to the parent-teacher conferences and all of those
> school-related activities alone. Out of the thirty-odd parents
> who show up at school functions, there will only be one or two
> fathers. It's because fathers work, I'm told. Well, I just happen
> to know that most of the other mothers I see over at the school
> work too. In fact, the husband of one of the mothers I always
> see works the night shift and is home during the day. But he
> never comes with his wife to anything at the school.

Another mother told me that one evening when she got home from
work her "macho" (her word) husband angrily told her that a man
had been phoning and asking for her, and he demanded to know just
who this guy was and why he was calling her. She laughed nastily
when she reported her answer to me: "That *guy* is the principal at
the grammar school your daughter has been attending for the last six
years. That *guy* has been the principal at that school ever since the
first of your six children started going there."
The responsibility for taking care of the kids when they're sick
remains for most of us predicated on gender. According to psychologist Paula Englander-Golden, whose paper on the subject will soon
appear in *Women's Psychology Quarterly,* women are absent from
work more often than men, but not because they themselves are ill.
Although her survey found that a common belief is that women take

more sick leave than men because of menstrual pains, she says they actually stay home to care for a sick child or take a child to a doctor or dental appointment, but they say they're sick so they can get sick pay. Her study reveals that the full burden of caring for a sick child falls heavier on a working mother than on a working father, but that comes as no surprise to the majority of working mothers I know:

> I took so much time off work when the baby was sick and had to be hospitalized for pneumonia that once he started to get better I had to go back to work, so I took him to the sitter's while he was still sick, still weak. And when people would ask me how he was getting along and I'd tell them, they would say, "Where do you leave him when you work?" When I said I left him with a sitter, they were shocked. What kind of a mother leaves a sick baby with a sitter? I felt so guilty. But then I felt guilty anyway, because if I hadn't taken him out of the house every day when he had a cold this never would have happened.

As it turned out this young mother stayed home with her child so much that she used up all her sick leave. And then when a cold she had caught developed into pneumonia, she continued to work until she collapsed.

Sick kids, injured kids, troubled kids. Most women know what I'm talking about. They know the stab of fear when the school nurse or the sitter calls at the office; the sense of apprehension when it is the principal; they know the guilt—the sense that somehow whatever it is wouldn't be if they were home where they belong. And on top of it all it's entirely up to these women to do whatever is required to make things right. It is a responsibility hidden from view by old and new motherhood myths alike.

What about single working mothers? Some single mothers, I've found, fare admirably. One woman told me that she missed the company and support of another adult, but she didn't miss the sharing of the load because her husband had never shared it. Another told me, "Things are better now. With my husband out of the picture, there's less tension—he was such a picky bastard that he got on everyone's nerves, and I found myself being drained because I was the peacemaker."

One of the most telling comments came from Jane, a thirty-five-year-old mother of two children:

Other than the money problems I have, it's really a lot easier than you might believe. Now that I'm no longer married, I don't feel the pressure to cook full-course dinners every night, nor the pressure to keep a spotless house, and the resentment that he who expects it plays golf every Saturday.

The kids and I sometimes have soup and sandwiches or scrambled eggs. We keep the house relatively neat, but I don't give it a major cleaning every week. And there's one less person to do laundry for, fewer dishes to wash, obviously, and no one to point out to me that the windows need washing.

This woman's remarks remind me of those of another woman who came up to speak to me after I'd given a talk at one of our local bookstores a number of years ago. When she explained that she was divorced and raising three children, I said something to the effect that because motherhood was tough enough for married women, I didn't know how single mothers managed to meet all the demands. She laughed and said, "I see your situation as little different than mine. With the exception of the lucky few who are married to unusual men, we are *all* really single mothers, whether we are married or not. Some of us have husbands, some of us have boyfriends, some of us have no men in our lives. But that is, as separate and apart from our being mothers as what our outside jobs may be."

And there are many discouraging stories. The most striking example I could cite is a co-worker—a single mother—whom I had to take to the psychiatric ward at Stanford Hospital when she broke down before the astonished eyes of us all. I later learned that the diagnosis was "nervous exhaustion." As it turned out, part of her problem was that she had been so forcefully programmed to believe that a husband was absolutely essential to her very survival that two years of being without one had culminated in her breakdown—she had panicked that she'd never find another one.

Feminine Mystique—Alive and Well

When you look for just what it is that so programmed this woman, you find out what it is that programs all of us who remain housewives even if we spend forty hours a week in an office: the feminine mystique. However obsolete and absurd the mystique may seem, it is still very much alive.

The mystique, as you may recall, is an extension of the Judeo-Christian ethic that holds patriarchy to be the ideal setup for families. It carries to ridiculous extremes the tradition that holds males to be superior to females, a man as the head of the household, a woman as the submissive keeper of it. It supports the patriarchal notion that the capstone of every woman's life is marriage and motherhood, that the ideal woman is totally dependent on her husband, and that her major interest is catching a man and keeping him. Where patriarchy is simple tradition, the mystique glorifies it all, maintaining that being a wife and mother is always wonderful, and parenting and housework are not only easy and natural for women, but oceans of fun. In short, the mystique holds the measure of a woman's worth to be how well she performs in housekeeping, mothering, and husband-pleasing. To be feminine is synonymous with excelling in these womanly functions, while not to excel or to disdain them is evidence of a lack of femininity.

As Betty Friedan explains in *The Feminine Mystique* (1963) the mystique was the creation of male advertising executives and magazine editors who had returned from the armed services after World War II. While in the trenches these men recalled in exaggerated form the warm hearths of the traditional homes they had grown up in. When they came home and resumed their old jobs, they recreated their idealized versions of the wife/mother old-fashioned home. The magazines sold the whole package of glorified housewifery. Their accomplice was the most forceful persuader ever devised: television, which sold the image in its commercials and its programming, brainwashing an entire nation into believing that a woman's place is in the home, where she is fulfilled and feminine in her "natural role."

Prior to the war attitudes about women's roles had been changing. Before Johnny went marching off, the small family had become prevalent, and the magazines of the day reflected women's dreams of having options beyond marriage and motherhood. Perhaps those males who shaped the mystique didn't like that trend. Another contributing factor was undoubtedly the need to push women, who had been moved into the factory to replace the men who had gone to war, back into the home to make room for our returning servicemen. Moreover, once those factories stopped making weapons for the war effort and their technology was turned to making appliances, those appliances had to be sold, and the market created for their use would have to be homemakers.

The selling of housewifery and motherhood at that time was responsible for the *intense* social pressure brought to bear on all normal people to marry and have children, and the more children they had the more normal they were—even patriotic as well as super-virtuous. The mystique mandated not only what the Bible mandates, but also a number of things it doesn't: A woman must be fulfilled as a career-housewife, prepare gourmet meals on her electric stove, sew on her machine, use Downy in the wash water, wax the floor with Brand A, wash the windows with Brand B, belong to a car pool, and look as if she stepped out of the pages of *Vogue* when her husband gets home from work each evening.

Although some people disbelieve it, what the mystique mandated in postwar America is not obsolete, which is why there are still women who fall apart at the seams when their marriages cave in and why, I repeat, many of us, no matter that we have learned to stand up on our own two feet, continue running in place. The double standard this mystique perpetuated remains in the very air we breathe and now, paradoxically, coexists with myths of career fulfillment. Even some very young women I have talked to who have never heard the term "the feminine mystique" try to live it, as reflexively as a fish swims. And married working wives, all running in place, try to emulate the television and magazine models of homemakers and keepers of the family's health and happiness.

The burden falls heaviest on the woman who feels that, although she must, she shouldn't work outside the home, and therefore feels guilty about it. Her guilt drives her, as she labors to excel in the home and do as much for her husband and children as she can. Another forceful spur to the weary back of some working housewives is that remnant of the patriarchy and the mystique that has made the approval of males central to our existence. Women who are married to men who see well-tended homes as an indication of feminine virtue and give their wives strokes or withhold them accordingly have a deep need to perform well. It is a terrible bind—to be exhausted from trying to do everything, to know in your heart it's so unfair, and also to feel that approval (and possibly love) will be withheld if you're not superhuman. Clearly this is a crazy-making situation for women caught up in it. And while there are those who are indifferent to what it means to individual women, there exists grave concern from those who have studied the matter. In 1981, for example, after reporting findings nearly identical to those of other studies that revealed most working mothers carry enormous burdens, the Worldwatch Institute grimly predicted that unless this situation changes or working mothers get some help or some relief, most of them the world over will eventually drop from exhaustion.

For a number of years now concern has been expressed that as more women enter the labor force in the same hard-paced professions as men, we might well see an increase in the stress-related diseases that strike men—in particular, heart disease. The good news, according to Susanne G. Haynes of the University of North Carolina at Chapel Hill, is that childless single and married women working in demanding careers suffer the lowest incidence of stress-related disease of all men *and* women studied. The bad news, according to Haynes, a research assistant professor in epidemiology, is that the highest incidence of heart disease, beating out men with their paltry 12.8 percent, occurs in women who are mothers and who hold down clerical jobs, with a percentage of 21.3. Haynes also found that those women who developed heart disease were those who were more likely not to express anger on the job or complain. In other words, those who were more forcefully conditioned than others to be submissive. As reported by Carol Kleiman (*Chicago Tribune,* August 2, 1982), Haynes concluded that, "Perhaps demands on the job, coupled with demands at home, explain the high incidence of heart disease among working women with several children." Perhaps?

That women may crack under the strain is obviously of major concern. But of equal, and perhaps even greater, concern is that the real losers in this situation are the children we Americans profess to love. In my view we don't love them at all. If as a society we did, would we permit the one person—the mother—designated as the caretaker of the children to be as abused as she currently is?

One woman I spoke to expressed the feelings I've had and the feelings others have reported to me when she said, "I cannot handle even one more thing, no matter what it is—large, small, important, trivial." As she spoke I remembered that I had left a blazer at the dry cleaner for six months because picking it up was "just one more thing." I also remember, with deep shame, resisting taking a seriously injured child—a child I would lay down my life for—to the emergency room for the same reason. "It's just a cut," I told myself, about a gash that required over one hundred stitches. Just one more thing. I took my son for treatment, of course, but looking back, it frightens me that being so overwhelmed caused me to resist the critical needs of the moment. And because of that incident I know that if there is any truth to the allegation that working mothers neglect their children, the guilty party is the society that keeps them running in place.

While the welfare of one's children can never be one of them, making sacrifices for a career of one's choosing is tolerable. Making those same bone-wearying sacrifices without the rewards of a career is something else entirely. And there's not one ordinary working mother I know in this very position who doesn't regret not having seen the handwriting on the wall. As one woman in her early thirties told me:

> I wish I'd paid more attention to the women's movement when I was a kid. I wish I'd thought about the distinct possibility that I'd *have* to work for the rest of my life. Then I could have prepared myself to do something besides pounding a typewriter all day. If I was doing something I *cared* about, then I might not be so depressed all the time in addition to being so tired. And if I'd really prepared myself for a career, the chances are I'd be making more money and I'd be less tired simply because I could afford to have someone come in and clean my house for me.

Betty Friedan called the feminine mystique "the problem that has no name." I call it the problem that won't go away. The media barrage that advertises it continues unabated, for the most part. Television still gives us mothers who are fully dressed, right down to their high-heeled shoes, at eight in the morning, going nowhere, cooking sausages, eggs, and pancakes for their children. Mothers still put Band-Aids on cut knees in the afternoon, something that working mothers see them do at nine o'clock at night—if they have time to watch television. "Ladies who've learned" still trust Crisco, and ladies who are still learning are instructed in the fine art of producing whiter than white washes by males whose voice-overs tell them how. Housewives with nothing to do, because being a housewife is such a snap, hang around the supermarket and squeeze the Charmin, while housewives with something better to do wax their sixty-foot elegant kitchen floors in just five minutes. All mothers are always available and always cleaning house, cooking, diapering darling babies, engaging in in-depth conversations with one another about detergents, bleaches, baby formulas, and floor wax. The only discernible attempt to reflect the existence of working women in modern life that I've seen is a commercial that shows a gorgeous woman changing from her work clothes to a glamorous gown who croons about bringing home the bacon and frying it up in a pan.

The mystique, obviously, is quite undead. And despite the evidence that most American women cannot stay home because inflation means they must work full-time, staying home is what the Religious New Right is promoting to save the American family. The aggrandized patriarchy is the ideal. The New Right, moreover, ever oblivious to reality, seeks to carve the patriarchal formula into legislative stone. Their agenda is contained in the Family Protection Act, drafted and boosted by the Moral Majority and its friends, which would *legislate* man as the head of the family and woman in the home. Not satisfied that such has been *culturally* ordained, the New Right has the goal of making it a matter of law.

Those who stand in the way of such a proposal are those who have seen the feminine mystique or the patriarchal ideal as a blueprint for madness and have dismissed it out of hand. Some over the years have become aware that there really exist no choices—that having children not only inhibits a woman's chances for a career of her choosing, but also virtually guarantees that she will have to work whether she wants to or not—and have opted for nonparenthood. Others who are aware of the problems have simply refused to go along with the idea that if they are married mothers they must also be domestic, husband-pleasing goddesses. However the resistance to adherence is expressed, those who have resisted or do resist are identified by the New Right as immoral and anti-family and are lumped together in the literature of the Moral Majority with pornographers and communists.

This indictment, of course, ignores the fact that feminists condemn pornography for the simple reason that it is exploitive of women. But then, when you consider Jerry Falwell's views on equality, you get a glimmer of how little either reality or fidelity to the word matters to the zealot who can always justify any position he takes in the name of God. For example, Jerry Falwell tells us that he is not opposed to equality for women, but just to a constitutional amendment that would guarantee it because "it strikes at the very foundation of our social structure. By mandating absolute equality," he says, we would "actually take away many of the special rights women now enjoy."

The sensible person asks, "What special rights?"

The zealot responds: "A definite violation of holy scripture, ERA defies the mandate that 'the husband is the head of the wife, even as Christ is the head of the Church' (Ephesians 5:23)."

In other words, the "special right" to be dominated by a husband. Not only are you expected to believe these are "special rights" because some disciple set them down in the Bible hundreds of years ago and Falwell has given them his own special interpretation, you are also required to believe the rest of the absolutes deriving from his questionable interpretation of the Scriptures: All men and women must accept Jesus Christ as their savior, and all must enter into holy matrimony and have children. The husband, as we know, will be the leader and the provider, and the wife will do as she's told. This absolute applies across the board to all people, regardless of their interpretations of the Bible, their present religious affiliations, marital status, or sexual persuasion. If they are not Christian, but Jewish, for example, they must convert; if they are not married, they must one day be; if they happen to be homosexual, they must be "cured" of this "sinful perversion"; if they have not as yet had children, they must have them at some future time; if they cannot have biological children, they should adopt. They will make a family and keep a Christian home according to God's holy order as it is defined by the Religious New Right.

The reason for these absolutes, according to Falwell, goes beyond salvation. The family, he says, is "the basic unit," the very foundation of this nation. Without this "basic unit," our nation will fall apart. All of this, according to Fundamentalist thought, is spelled out very concisely in the Bible. Capitalism is something that was bestowed upon this nation at its inception. Communism, on the other hand, is Satan's plan in action. Lest any of you believe that the New Right's concern for the family has anything to do with the quality of life for its individual members, it must be understood that the family

—"the basic unit"—is but a device, or the glue that holds the divinely ordained capitalism together. Without the family it is capitalism and hence the nation that will go down the tubes.

To keep this from happening, feminism, which rejects the notion of male superiority and the validity of patriarchy, must be contained. Whether it is healthy or not for individual families, "traditional values" must be restored, even if restoration depends on *force*. Anything for the cause.

And "anything for the cause" means marching under the pro-family banner while labeling anyone who disagrees with New Right absolutes as anti-family. It means identifying feminism as the enemy of the family and the cause of our spiraling divorce rate, while ignoring the distinct possibility that its genuine cause may be the early marriages and the giddy standards the feminine mystique gave us. It means ignoring the established fact that the mystique proved not just to be unhealthy for marriage, but not really good for mothers and the multitudes of children they produced. As Betty Friedan noted in her book, the pressures it created drove women to alcoholism, drug abuse, child abuse, mental breakdown, and suicide, none of which is exactly conducive to wholesome family life. Numerous studies have since borne out Friedan's early work; in *The Future of Marriage,* published in 1972, sociologist Jessie Bernard warned that the traditional nuclear family was leading to mental illness and divorce; then in 1975, in *The Future of Motherhood,* she warned that the burdens heaped on mothers would lead to the demise of the family.

In the rest of this book I intend to show that not only is the New Right dead wrong in identifying feminism as the villain, but that Dr. Bernard's words are proving to be prophetic. I also intend to demonstrate that as bad as the situation for women currently is, if this New Right movement gets its way, the situation will get worse: If the New Right succeeds in its objectives, we will never have equality under the law; working, however necessary, will carry with it some sort of stigma; and our "place" in society will perpetually remain something to be determined by males who have power over our lives.

Of course while the New Right superstars and their minions point disapproving fingers at all working women, accusing them of either gross materialism or hedonism, they *do* acknowledge that some women must work to avoid going on welfare. Their primary objections to women working outside the home seem to focus on women who try to help the family to get ahead or who are committed to a profession. Their protests grow louder when a woman works outside the home for self-actualization. They object to women having careers on the basis that they will be less devoted to the patriarchal ideal. This being the case, I would speculate that a goal of the New Right is to return us to a tradition that closes off the opportunities that now exist for women to enter into the professions. Perhaps they have in mind some discriminatory laws to reinforce those that already exist.

But worse than anything else, the number one goal on the New Right agenda is to deny women the right of reproductive freedom of choice. In the next two chapters all of the ramifications of this dubious goal will be covered in detail. For now it is enough to say that if the New Right is successful, we will return to that tragic dark age when women were forced to have one child after another until it killed them.

This, then, and much more, is what the New Right that calls itself pro-family has in mind for us.

In breathing new life into the feminine mystique, is their goal the preservation of the American family? Or is it something else? The fact that the feminine mystique—which turned women into baby-makers and thing-buyers seemingly interested only in aggrandizing their homes and looking feminine—created unprecedented prosperity was lost on no one. This may be the reason it never entirely faded away. If capitalism is perceived as being divinely ordained, then surely making profits must put those who make them in a state of divine grace, and thus the mystique could be perceived as divinely ordained as well. Where the New Right's interest in turning you into a baby-maker really lies, I leave up to you to decide after you review the evidence to be presented in the chapters that follow.

Betty Friedan has stated that the second stage of feminism is for the lambs to sit down with the lions. But when I stand back and take a long look, I can only conclude that the agenda of the lions is to return us to the traditions of the 1900s, when the patriarchy ruled unchallenged, and the baby-makers were not allowed to own property nor permitted to vote.

I submit, therefore, that the second stage of feminism is *not* to sit down with the very people who have declared war on our rights but to finish the job Friedan started when she put the feminine mystique on trial two decades ago: give it the coup de grace and do it before the New Right has a chance to revive it in the form of *legislated* patriarchy.

II

WHOSE BODY IS IT, ANYWAY?

Such Crazy Legislation Could Never Pass

One of the first of my rituals to get chucked after I went to work full-time was having a second cup of coffee in the morning and reading the newspaper. Another was watching the evening news on television. I was thus left with only those bits and pieces of news that came through my car radio on the way to and from work to provide me with a sketchy view of what was going on in the world. I knew, of course, that in 1980 we had elected a new president. I was vaguely aware that a number of liberal and moderate legislators in our Congress had been voted out of office, and even more vaguely aware that the reason for most of the upsets had to do with the Religious New Right having targeted pro-choice candidates for defeat, running surprisingly effective and successful campaigns against them.

But I wasn't terribly upset, as I, like most working mothers, had the immediate concerns of my day-to-day life in a pressure cooker: whether Senators Church or Bayh or McGovern had or had not been returned to the Senate was inconsequential as compared to more critical personal matters such as what to cook for dinner and how to get it all served before going over to the school for open house, for instance.

Then I quit my job. And then I started reading the newspaper again.

And when, on May 22, 1981, I opened up my morning paper and saw the headline, I almost choked on my second cup of coffee as I read that the United States Senate had voted in favor of an appropriations bill with a rider attached to it that would allow Medicaid abortions *only* to save a woman's life, but for no other reason—not even when pregnancy was the result of rape or incest. I couldn't believe it. Barefoot and pregnant as I had been from too much housewifery and mothering—and exhausted from too much working—I had been unaware that such was even under discussion. But then as I read on and learned that a vote on the issue had not been expected, I realized that I wasn't the only one who had been asleep.

Still, I couldn't believe it. This piece of legislation not only meant that women who happened to be poor and had had contraceptive failures or had been simply careless would be penalized by being forced to continue an unwanted pregnancy; it also meant that young girls who were victims of rape or incest, on top of having endured the trauma of having been assaulted, would be forced to give birth to children.

Reading on, I learned that legislators had been caught up short, as this rider had been tacked on by Senator Jesse Helms, an avowed supporter of the so-called "pro-life" lobby and member of the Fundamentalist fringe, and that a number of legislators had succumbed to pressure from the right-to-life movement, which had grown considerably since the last time I'd paid much attention to it. Where once it had consisted primarily of the National Right-to-Life Committee, which was predominantly Catholic, it now comprised a coalition that was overwhelmingly non-Catholic and that included the Moral Majority and all of its affiliate organizations, the Mormon Church, Stop ERA, the American Life Lobby, and various and sundry Fundamentalist church organizations—the coalition that had targeted moderate and liberal legislators for defeat over one single issue—freedom to choose as set down by the United States Supreme Court.

I was shocked that this group could be successful, but not especially shocked, after I had thought about it, that they would be indifferent to the plight of poor women generally and victims of rape and incest in particular. They have a peculiar view, expressed quite well by Congressman Henry Hyde, who justified his staunch anti-choice position on the grounds that rape rarely resulted in pregnancy, so such should not be a consideration in passing "pro-life" legislation. But, as Senator Edward Kennedy said in response, "That's small comfort to the woman it happens to."

And it does happen. Tom Braden, a political commentator and the father of eight children, gives us an idea of what it might be like when he tells us the story of what happened to one of his daughters a few years ago after she left a Fourth of July celebration in Washington. In his piece (July 1981) he says that his child was seized by three men who held her to the floor of a car:

> She was tied, gagged, and taken to a house . . . for the rest of the night . . . [where] she was repeatedly beaten and raped. The next morning she was blindfolded and driven back to the Monument grounds and shoved out of the car. Eventually, sometime about midday, she made her way home.
> . . . [W]ithin a very short time, my daughter knew she was pregnant.
> Now, I would like to ask Senator Helms what he would do if he had been the father of the girl. I know what I did. And I can promise the senator and the Moral Majority and the shrill voices of the Right-to-Life movement that no matter what law they pass and how stringent the penalty, I would do it again.

It is hard to say what Senator Helms might do under similar circumstances, but I can tell you what one daughter of parents who possess his narrow view did. When she was just twelve years old, this girl told me, she was forcibly raped while on a family vacation. It was in the morning, and she had slipped out early to take a stroll along the beach. The man who raped her, she said, was about twenty-five years old. No, she had never told anyone about it—least of all her church-going parents, because she was certain they would beat her. For months after the rape she jumped at her own shadow,

had the shakes, and couldn't tolerate being alone. When I asked her
what she would have done if she had got pregnant as a result of the
rape, she told me, "I just would have run away. I just would have
given the baby up for adoption and afterward called my parents and
begged them to forgive me."

She would have begged her parents to forgive her for having been
assaulted. The piety of her parents was responsible for this child having to suffer her trauma alone. And this is the mentality, Tom Braden warns, that would be imposed on us all. In the same piece in
which he discusses his daughter, he writes of this legislation that
Helms bullied through.

> . . . [It] was not a question of cutting the budget. Abortion
> costs for poor women who are raped do not amount to that
> much.
>
> Rather, it was a question of morality. Republican Senator
> Jesse Helms of North Carolina and the Moral Majority which
> follows him around are convinced that abortion is wrong even
> when the woman who wants one wants it because she has been
> raped.
>
> So I don't think it will be very long before Jesse and his
> friends are going to come after the unpoor, that is to say after
> you and me and our daughters.
>
> In this instance I am not very comfortable about being un-
> poor. . . . I reason that by the same standard with which the
> senators dealt with the poor, they will shortly deal with
> me. . . .

Having been awakened by a headline I found shocking, I immediately learned that Tom Braden's concern was far from unfounded.
Jesse Helms has his Human Life Bill, and Senator Orrin Hatch of
Utah, who is a devout Mormon, has his Human Life Amendment,
and both of them, along with their friends in the Moral Majority, the
Mormon Church, the National Right-to-Life Committee, and all of
the rest of the far right, old and new, are anxious for either one of
these measures to become a matter of law. The measure that out-
lawed Medicaid abortions for poor women probably was just the
warm-up for the main event, which would outlaw them for everyone
else.

Either of these pieces of legislation would not simply take us back to the days before the United States Supreme Court ruled, but would grant fertilized eggs full personhood from the moment of conception, thereby making anyone who participated in an abortion, including the mother, subject to charges of premeditated murder. In fact, "accomplices" would consist of anyone who might lend a woman money for an abortion and anyone who might drive her to a clinic to obtain one. Such legislation would also mandate the investigation of all miscarriages, and a woman who had not taken proper care of herself might be found guilty of neglect.

It would also outlaw "morning after" birth control pills, IUD's, or any form of birth control that prevents a fertilized egg from attaching itself to the uterine wall. It would even ban radiation therapy for cancer patients suspected of being pregnant and could quite possibly result in restrictions on women in their work places, because employers could be held liable should anything happen to an unborn fetus if it could be demonstrated that the work place had a damaging effect on it.

But such crazy legislation could never pass. Don't count on it—crazy legislation has already passed, as we saw on May 22, 1981. Furthermore, our legislators are not only pressured by the Moral Majority, the "pro-life" lobby, and other groups, but their offices are flooded each week with thousands and thousands of letters from citizens who are opposed to abortion on moral grounds. And I am very concerned that many letter writers are unaware of the ramifications of the legislation they tell their representatives and senators they are in favor of. This concern is based on the answers I got when I asked three different conservative Christian women these questions: Are you opposed to the termination of a pregnancy to save the life of a mother? In the event of incest or rape? In the event that the child would be hideously deformed and not really a child at all? The answers from all three to all three questions were, "No, No, No." And when I asked, "Are you aware that the Human Life Amendment or the Human Life Bill would prohibit terminations in those instances, again, the answer was, "No." Finally, when I asked if they would support legislation that would prohibit abortion in these instances, they said, "No." This certainly tells me that there must be people who do not fully understand the legislation they may urge their congressman to pass.

Jesse Helms, Orrin Hatch, Henry Hyde, Jerry Falwell, Phyllis Schlafly, and all of their lieutenants and foot soldiers, and even the President of the United States, who press for this very rigid sort of legislation say they do so because they have a "deep reverence for human life," and they say that they believe abortion is murder. In other areas where they would like to restrict our freedoms, they say it is their concern for the collapse of the family, the decline in morality of our youth, or whatever reason may be handy, wholesome sounding, and can be stated as a quick and snappy homily or one-liner. But whatever they say, the true agenda, as pertains to *female bodies only,* is spelled out in various and sundry pieces of legislation such as the Family Protection Act, chastity bills, and proposed rules and regulations that various right-wing legislators try to work in here and there. Pulled together from the various proposals that exist as of this writing, summed up, this is the agenda:

- A ban on abortion under any circumstances, and prohibition of certain forms of birth control.

- A requirement that parents of minors be informed within ten days after their daughters have received prescriptions for birth control pills, or other forms of contraception that would require a prescription.

- Elimination of sex education in the public schools on the grounds that sex-educators encourage teenage sexual activity and teach their students how to masturbate and teach perversion.

- As an interim device, "Informed Consent" laws that would require a medical practitioner to spell out in living color precisely each detail of an abortion to a woman who is scheduled to have one, and would require that after this is spelled out, she wait twenty-four hours before undergoing the procedure.

This last agenda item has little to do with what it calls itself: "Informed Consent." It has, instead, to do with persuading a woman not to have an abortion and making it as difficult as possible under current law for her to do so. Most affected will be women who have to travel from rural areas to cities, as the time, arrangements to leave work, and the cost of transportation will be doubled.

While these measures would certainly affect all women, they seem to be designed to punish unmarried young females by exposing them to pregnancy and denying them access to abortion. The males who would impregnate them would be untouched, while young girls would be forced to bear the scars for the rest of their lives.

Women who value their freedom had better read closely as they open their morning papers.

Locked into Poverty

Immediately punished, of course, are poor women. It is my guess that even as of this moment many of them have no idea that should they find themselves with an unplanned pregnancy, however it occurs, they will be conscripted into childbirth. This, we know, is discrimination. But the word *discrimination* is woefully inadequate to describe the consequences. The one thing that locks a woman into a cycle of poverty more than anything else is not being able to control her own reproduction. In case after case of welfare mothers, the trouble began with the first unplanned pregnancy and got worse with each subsequent one. Here we are, not providing sufficient services in the first place, as evidenced by the welfare rolls, and the New Right wants to snatch back what little exists.

An account in the September 27, 1981, "This World" section of the *San Francisco Chronicle* fully illustrates how lack of education and services can lock a woman into life-long poverty. At 57 Louise Lowman (as she is called in the article) is said to be "typical." She has been on welfare for thirty-five years, since she became pregnant for the first time. Up until that point in her life the future had looked bright. She had come from a loving, modest-income family—not on welfare—and she had done well in school. After graduating from high school she had planned to become a nurse. But her dreams and her plans were dashed because her parents could not afford to send her to college. She worked at a few menial jobs, always thinking that she could and would do better. The one good thing in her otherwise dismal life was her boyfriend. Just a few weeks after he had been drafted into the army, twenty-two-year-old Louise discovered she was pregnant. There was nothing she could do but have the baby and go on welfare. Thus began a cycle of poverty and degradation culminating in a total of ten children, whom Louise has raised in a cramped, rat-infested apartment with never enough food to go around.

Of the ten children, five have managed to escape from the Chicago ghetto where they grew up, one is retarded, one is still in high school, and three are adults on welfare. One of these three has now presented her mother with a grandchild who is on his way to becoming the third generation in the welfare cycle that started with Louise—a cycle that quite possibly never would have got started in the first place had Louise Lowman been given full access to birth control information and family planning services, and one that might not have been perpetuated had some social worker somewhere along the line suggested to Louise that she attempt to control her own fertility.

Another woman whose case illustrates how early the cycle can start was profiled in an article in the *San Francisco Chronicle* (October 23, 1981). The Oakland Housing Authority said she was too young to be able to rent her own apartment. Not yet seventeen at the time, she was the mother of three children with one more on the way.

The Moral Majority, of course, would dismiss the plight of this young mother by saying that this unmarried girl should not have sex, and one of their goals in seeking to have legislation passed denying contraceptives to minors is to keep them chaste. Obviously fear of pregnancy isn't enough of a deterrent. While I believe that restraint in young people is a good idea, if they are going to be sexually active, they ought to have whatever protection they need. The moralistic attitude of "Well, she made her bed, let her lie in it" ignores the fact that when a young girl does indeed "lie in it" young innocents do so with her, and the price that society pays doesn't end with the welfare dollar.

When I read stories about mothers like Louise and the young mother denied housing, and I read them all too often, I despair of what will become of the children. There is little likelihood that they will have any chance at all for a decent life, and every likelihood that the females among them will do as their mothers did. It is painful to think of the misery that is yet to settle in on this girl—a girl my own daughter's age—the mother of three and expecting another, and what life will be like for her in the future. It deeply saddens me that Louise Lowman, who is "typical," has had, and continues to have, such a wretched life. It saddens me all the more because if we really wanted to, we could wipe out much of the poverty in the United States, and save millions of tax dollars in the bargain, if we would just do the one obvious thing: *Make it both desirable and possible for all women to control their own fertility.*

The young woman denied housing seems all that much more a victim because she did not want to get pregnant in the first place—she had been taking birth control pills each and every time she got pregnant—but when she told her doctor she wanted to have a tubal ligation after her next birth because the pills apparently didn't work, he told her she was too young. Not too young to be a mother of four? And perhaps even more in the near future? Whose body is it we're talking about, anyway? (Needless to say it strikes me as very strange that her doctor allowed this girl to continue with contraception that was apparently ineffective for her.)

If I ruled the social welfare system, it would be *law* that every female of child-bearing age be provided with a completely unvarnished job description of parenthood in advance and every possible option to control her own fertility. Furthermore, I would see to it that the law would provide, regardless of one's race or economic status, those who did not wish to become pregnant in the future with the means to obtain a tubal ligation. My law would provide that the same funds as would be given her for a dependent child to age eighteen be guaranteed to that woman for eighteen years following her surgery. The savings in tax dollars would be astronomical. The savings in human despair, impossible to measure.

Of course extremists at either end of the spectrum would object. In one corner we have the moralist, the self-appointed keeper of our virtue, presiding over the bodies of poor women, denying them the right not to have children without providing them with the means to care for them. And in the other corner we have a certain brand of liberal who wants to "protect" poor women from being "forced" to control their own fertility. These are the ones who accuse such agencies as Planned Parenthood of racism every time they try to reach out to help women avoid having unwanted children that they can neither afford nor are prepared to parent. Lunacy on both sides of the equation is what will keep the Louise Lowmans of this country proliferating in abject misery.

True discrimination against the poor, no matter what its ethical origins, usually shows itself as a general indifference to their plight. In Margaret Sanger's day many of the affluent women who were involved in her crusade to bring birth control to America raised their well-groomed eyebrows when Sanger wanted to set up clinics for poor women. Their attitude was one of "Whatever for? The poor will always have problems." Today the same indifference is seen in the so-called pro-life groups. Discrimination is also evident in those who take a "liberal" position, such as *San Francisco Chronicle* columnist Charles McCabe, who perpetually accuses Planned Parenthood of discriminating against the poor, "especially racial minorities," as he put it on October 19, 1981. McCabe and those who think as he does are just as guilty of indifference as those well-bred women Margaret Sanger had to deal with, as it is this very attitude that works to oppress while it inflames. McCabe's thesis is, of course, that the white middle class in Planned Parenthood have in mind "racial genocide" to keep the black population down and therefore keep them from having any political clout.

Abortion is murder, family planning is genocide. Simplistic thinking is ever operational at both extremes of the political spectrum, but caught in the crunch are women whose bodies aren't their own, but instead mere vessels to reproduce the species. Militant blacks like Dick Gregory who talk about political power in the numbers of children they'd have (force their women to have?) and raise the question of "genocide" are just as guilty of sexism as Jerry Falwell. Black or white, rich or poor, we women are diminished as persons. And the charge of genocide is ludicrous.

Shirley Chisholm knocked out that foolishness and simultaneously knocked out another foul myth—that poor black women *want* to have lots of babies so they can collect the welfare dollar—back in 1969 when as a Congresswoman she told the Senate Committee on Labor and Public Welfare:

> I know that in my own Bedford-Stuyvesant community black women are glad to get direction in the area of family planning. I know that thousands of black women have been maimed by botched abortions because they couldn't get family planning help that white women could get. I have heard some repercussions that family planning is a form of genocide. But the people this would affect—in Harlem and Bedford-Stuyvesant—

think otherwise. I have had hundreds of black women come to see me over the past ten years because they want family planning.

I have but one answer for anyone who dares to accuse anyone else of racism solely on the basis of her (or his) desire to make family planning available to *all* women: It is not easy to be a mother, often even under the best of circumstances. I speak from experience when I say that, and I speak from experience when I say it isn't easy to be a working mother, as so many of us are these days. But I cannot imagine much that could be worse than subsisting at the poverty level while having little control over how many times I might again become a mother. All the young woman who was denied housing can look forward to is a life of being deprived, demeaned, and degraded by an inadequate system (growing more inadequate every day), while being overwhelmed with the burdens of having too many children too soon and too young. She is but one of millions of American *women* so condemned.

Furthermore, extreme liberals who cry genocide wind up giving the New Right another weapon for their inflammatory arsenal. According to Gloria Steinem they use it to assert that legalized abortion has moved us one step closer to compulsory abortion for "undesirables." Both sides seem to ignore the fact that legalized abortion has unquestionably cut down on the number of deaths from botched abortion. In Harlem Hospital alone, reports Steinem, there were 750 fewer admissions for botched abortions following the 1971 liberation of New York State law.

A Foolish Debate

While there may exist no doubt in the minds of the anti-choice fanatics that human life begins at the very split second of conception, there does exist some doubt in the minds of those who really might know. When one authority on such matters, Yale University geneticist Dr. Leon Rosenberg, was asked his opinion, he told the Senate Committee:

The crux of the bill before you is the statement that "present-day scientific evidence indicates a significant likelihood that human life exists from conception." I must respectfully but firmly disagree with this statement for two reasons: first because I know of no scientific evidence which bears on the question of when actual human life exists; second because I believe that the notion embodied in the phrase, "actual human life" is not a scientific one, but rather a philosophical and religious one.

There is no reason to debate or doubt the scientific evidence indicating that conception is a critical event in human reproduction (which establishes the potential for the development of human life).

When does this potential for human life become actual? I do not know. Moreover, I have not been able to find a single piece of scientific evidence which helps me with the question.

In an article in *Newsweek* (January 11, 1982), Jerry Adler and John Carey point out the little-talked-about fact that "between one half and two thirds of fertilized eggs will fail to implant themselves in the uterus and will be washed away unnoticed." It is a statistic, they say, that not even a Constitutional amendment will alter. While these fertilized eggs are unquestionably alive, the question is, are they persons?

Dr. Malcolm Potts, the executive director of the International Fertility Research Program, located in North Carolina, offers still another view—and one worth paying very close attention to. He tells us, for example, that a woman has nearly seven million eggs, but during her lifetime only four hundred will be ovulated. The testes manufacture almost two hundred million sperm each day. "Why this apparent waste?" he asks. And then he answers his own question: It is necessary because of the way development works. Reproduction is not like an assembly line where a blueprint is turned invariably into a quality product. In nature's factory mistakes are common. Inspection and rejection must be uncompromising.

The female reproductive tract can be a hostile environment. Of the hundreds of millions of sperm deposited in the vagina, the majority never even get into the uterus. . . . Overcoming this obstacle course perhaps weeds out the 40 percent abnormal sperm that can occur in a healthy man's ejaculate.

Fertilization, the next step, is only the beginning of an uncertain and easily broken chain of events. Over the next five days, the fertilized egg—carrying genes from both the father and the mother—divides to become a blastocyst, or hollow ball of cells, about one fourth the size of the period at the end of this sentence. The dividing egg passes down the fallopian tube to enter the uterus, where it attaches to the wall, a step called implantation. The outer cells go on to form the placenta and the amniotic sac, and the inner ones, the embryo. But again, the process can go wrong.

Sometimes the embryo fails to develop any further though the placenta grows, resulting in a molar pregnancy. In rare cases the placenta becomes malignant. Such a cancer, or choriocarcinoma, can kill a woman rapidly.

In about one in 300 pregnancies, the human egg stops in its journey to the uterus and implants in the fallopian tube, producing an ectopic pregnancy. Rapid embryonic growth causes bleeding that endangers the woman's life unless surgical abortion is performed.

One curiosity of human development occurs without fertilization. A teratoma is a tumor that usually forms in the ovaries or testes and may contain a tooth, strands of hair, or fragments of a nervous system.

. . . Not all fertilized eggs grow into babies, and some tumors have several of the characteristics of fertilized eggs. Moreover, all through early development, there is a selective elimination of developmental errors. As few as 60 percent of early embryos survive to implantation. And perhaps fewer than half of these make it to the second week of pregnancy. More than half of a woman's conceptions may end before she is even aware of being pregnant. A substantial proportion of miscarriages involve defective embryos.

If the body did not eliminate most abnormal embryos, half or more of all babies born would be grossly abnormal . . . sometimes hideously incomplete. If nature fails to eliminate an abnormal pregnancy, should a doctor be allowed to do the job with an abortion? What happens to the argument that a genetically unique product of fertilization has the right to life when we consider that a cancer of the placenta is also genetically unique? Why does the Catholic church allow surgical abortion for an ectopic pregnancy but not for an intrauterine pregnancy, when each can produce a normal baby?

The answers to these questions go beyond the facts of biology, but the remarkable phenomena of early human development make it hard to apply uncompromising answers (*Science '82*, March 1982).

Dr. Potts's observations should be enough to convince anyone that matters of conception and pregnancy are best left to those who get pregnant and those who provide care for them. As a member of the former group who has placed trust in the latter, I am convinced that abstract debates about when human life begins are utterly irrelevant to reality, if not downright silly. But silly debates become serious when they threaten to change the law of the land. If I read the positions of the Religious New Right and Dr. Potts correctly, carried to its most absurd extreme, pro-life legislation could mean that *any woman could be legally obligated to endure a life-threatening carcinoma.*

Writing in the July 17, 1981, issue of *Science,* Brian G. Zack of the Department of Pediatrics at Rutgers Medical School argues against the passage of a prohibitive law from another point of view: "One of the basic functions of the law," he writes, "must be to identify those actions which are abhorrent to the community and outlaw them. Thus, murder, considered abhorrent by most members of most communities, is widely regarded by the law as the most serious of crimes." We currently have a consensus of opinion that holds that murder of an already born member of society is such an action; there exists no such consensus that abortion is tantamount to the same thing and, in fact, according to a *Washington Post*–ABC News Poll (June 8, 1981), seventy percent of all Americans believe that it isn't; they also believe that this should not be a matter of legislation.

Furthermore, it is very important to keep in mind that efforts to have a law enacted that states absolutely that life begins at conception totally disregards the beliefs of other major religions in this nation: those of some Protestant sects and of Jews, who do not hold that the "soul" comes into being at the moment of conception but rather that the spiritual and physical person come into being simultaneously at the moment of birth. As Raine Eisler, writing in the September–October 1981 issue of *The Humanist,* points out:

The incorporation into the highest law of the United States—our Constitution—of the theological position that human life begins at fertilization would constitute a radical departure from the First Amendment's guarantee of freedom of religion and separation of church and state. Many religious and secular leaders point out that the founders of this country included these principles in our Constitution to ensure that the combination of church and state, which in Europe led to terrible religious persecutions, could never come about here. They are particularly alarmed about passage of the HLA at a time when a tide of religious intolerance is gaining momentum and when, in the name of God, country, and morality, old and new hatreds and prejudices are being rekindled all over our land.

Who Owns Women's Bodies?

Regarding the implications of such legislation for the individual, Congressman Paul N. McCloskey said after passage of the restrictive and discriminatory Medicaid legislation, ". . . How would we (men) feel if a Congress made up of a majority of women were to vote mandatory vasectomies for all men who had sired two or more children?"

I think they would feel as if they had been raped—as if their bodies, which are supposed to be their own, had been violated just by the very idea of such legislation.

Their bodies are their bodies.

Well, *my* body is *my* body. It is not something to be encumbered with as many laws as might regulate the operation of my automobile; my body is not a vehicle for legislation. If I want to have my body medically treated, or if I choose not to, that is my right. I can have my nose bobbed, my face lifted, my tubes tied, my uterus removed. I can also refuse to have my uterus removed simply because some doctor thinks it's a good idea. No one can force me to have surgery that I don't want to have. If I want my body to get pregnant and give birth, that is a decision that I, and I alone, can make. If I don't want my body to give birth that should also be my decision. If I want to make my body fat or thin or if I neglect my body, that is my business. If I wish to *kill* my body, I consider that my right too.

My body became my own only recently. It has been mine only since the United States Supreme Court decreed in 1973 that it was. And since then the truth of the matter has become as clear as it ought to have been all along: No one should be able to control my body without my express permission. I'm still angry that it was ever otherwise. As recently as twelve years ago laws and hospital policies existed that would not allow me to have a necessary surgical procedure that would interfere with my fertility without my husband's written consent.

I became aware of this when a member of my family was taken by ambulance to the hospital, where it was determined that she would bleed to death if she did not have surgery immediately. Did the doctor perform the hysterectomy then and there? No. As she lay bleeding a search party was dispatched to find her husband. Presumably, had he not been found, or had he wanted to get rid of his wife and therefore refused to sign the consent form, she simply would have bled to death. Had that occurred she would have left behind a thirteen-year-old daughter who desperately needed her mother.

The same mind-set, peculiar to ultraconservative male thinking, is no doubt what is behind the far right's stated goal to cut off funding of shelters for battered wives. They say that they oppose tax dollars being used for such things and oppose the government interference in our personal lives that comes with those dollars. More likely, what they really oppose is interference in a man's right to beat up on his wife's body, which belongs not to her but to her husband.

Such a point of view is what is behind the Moral Majority's objection to the book *Our Bodies, Ourselves*. In the mailing campaign that called this book pornographic, the Moral Majority cited as pornographic the section of the book that instructed women in self-examination techniques. Since, in their view, our bodies aren't our own, we ought not be allowed to inspect them.

In response to this point of view, Sonia Johnson (*From Housewife to Heretic,* 1981) writes of the Mormon attitude:

> Something was sick about a society which fulsomely extolled motherhood but wouldn't even tell young women what aperture of their bodies babies issued from, as if we had no right to understand our own various orifices. It was as if somehow our bodies, and especially our sexual organs, didn't ultimately be-

long to us at all, and that if we thought about them or touched them, we were trespassing upon someone else's property. Which, of course, is patriarchy's clear message to women. From the moment we're born female, our bodies belong to that faceless male who will one day marry us.

Men's bodies belong to themselves from the moment they are born male.

. . . I was being methodically reduced by my society to mere ovaries, womb, and vagina. Even taken all together, those parts make a very small, very limited, and very partial woman.

No wonder I was miserable.

With respect to reproductive freedom specifically, it must be remembered by those who doubt we are in danger of losing it that as recently as 1970 *all* forms of birth control were prohibited in Wisconsin and Massachusetts, and if a woman wanted the tubal ligation so easy to obtain today but happened to live in Utah, the law would prevent her from obtaining one. In California, even with her husband's consent, and even if she already had six children, a woman could not easily obtain a sterilization operation.

The first anti-choice laws were enacted in 1873, and they were very difficult to knock down. They are worth looking at because the wording of these laws instantly brings to mind the New Right philosophy as it is now being expressed, one hundred years later:

Every obscene, lewd, lascivious, or filthy book, pamphlet, picture, paper, letter, writing, print, or other publication of an indecent character; and

Every article or thing designed, adapted or intended for preventing conception or producing abortion, or for any indecent or immoral use; and

Every article, instrument, substance, drug, medicine, or thing which is advertised or described in a manner calculated to lead another to use or apply it for preventing conception or producing abortion, or for any indecent or immoral purposes; . . .

Every paper, writing, advertisement, or representation that any article, instrument, substance, drug, medicine, or thing may, or can, be used or applied for preventing conception or producing abortion, or for any indecent or immoral purposes . . .

Notice how pornography and the right to choose are lumped together as equally sinful. This is why when Jerry Falwell opens his mouth I think I've been swallowed up in a time warp.

Not only does the rhetoric of those times match what we are hearing today; so do the tactics. I see little difference between the tactics used by Senator Jesse Helms to get a restrictive abortion law on the books and the tactics used by Anthony Comstock, who was the director of the Society for the Suppression of Vice in 1873, to get his prohibitive law through. Helms tacked a rider onto an appropriations bill at the last minute, thereby denying his colleagues thoughtful consideration of the matter or any real debate. The law Comstock was sponsoring had to be passed before midnight, but when the deliberations started to go beyond that hour, Comstock merely had the clock stopped. The law was actually passed at 2:00 A.M.

Jesse Helms has stated that he will stop at nothing to get his Human Life Bill passed. I believe it.

Reversing archaic laws can take a very long time. Margaret Sanger spent decades trying to live under the Comstock laws while trying to get them reversed. Sanger was a nurse in the Brooklyn area in the early 1920s. What kept her fighting as hard as she did was the daily sight of women having too many children in succession and dying before they reached their middle years. She was further sickened at watching desperate women, denied contraception, die from self-inflicted abortions. She was determined to prevent such tragedies by bringing birth control to America, which she did. She published a newsletter explaining birth control to women (pornography, under Comstock's law), and she opened up birth-control clinics to provide women with the diaphragm. She also wound up in jail on more than one occasion.

We would do well to remember what Margaret Sanger did, not only because it led to our having the right to choose, but also because if the Religious New Right continues to be successful, history may well repeat itself. Like dominoes, one by one our rights to choose could be lost.

The possibility that my basic right to control my own body may be swept away tells me that every single one of my other rights is also in jeopardy. As Margaret Sanger said so long ago, "No woman will ever be free until she can choose whether or not to become a mother." I interpret that as meaning that beyond the very real restrictions that motherhood imposes on a woman's freedoms, if she is denied reproductive freedom of choice, she may be denied other freedoms as well. Is there a great difference in degree or quality between rescinding my right to control my own body and rescinding my right to vote, if the former is justified solely on the basis of my being female? We are already all too aware that the Religious New Right isn't interested simply in eliminating the freedom of women to choose but also is opposed to women having equality under the law. If you think I've lost my mind for believing that there also exists a desire to take away our right to vote, please be reminded of the frequently quoted words of Howard Phillips, a member of the Board of Directors of the Moral Majority and head of the Conservative Caucus:

> A second major result of policies that have been anti-family, that have begun not just in this decade or even in this century but have extended for many years, has been the liberation of the wife from the leadership of the husband. It has been a conscious policy of government to liberate the wife from the leadership of the husband and thus break up the family unit as a unit of government.
>
> First, in the 1800s, legislation was passed that gave women property rights. Second we saw how women were liberated from the leadership of their husbands politically. You know, it used to be that in recognition of the family as a basic unit of society we had one family one vote. And we have seen the trend instead toward one person one vote. . . .

These words were spoken in a speech to Citizens for Biblical Morality in the space age—in the year 1980. They were obviously spoken by a man and accepted by a group of people who believe that women are things, not citizens.

Things, whose bodies have but one function: to serve man. That, of course, is the rapist's view. The rapist needs no justification for his violation of others' rights beyond his belief that they are mere objects to be used for his sick gratification. Typically the rapist is incapable of feeling empathy, and those who are so lacking are generally diagnosed by psychologists as being sociopaths.

As Susan Brownmiller so vividly illustrates in her book *Against Our Will*, at the core of the rapist mentality is the view that women are property. And because they are property and not human beings, men pass the laws that would have a female who becomes pregnant punished for the crime perpetrated on her person. Brownmiller points out that this is because historically women have been perceived as being responsible for their own rapes—they are the guilty parties for having "sinfully" invited the act. Well, females as young as three months old and as old as ninety have been raped. Did they behave in a provocative manner, inviting sexual encounter? Besides, even if a rape victim is an attractive young woman, blaming her for the rape is tantamount to blaming a bank for a robbery: "Well, you see, your honor, the bank was there and it had all this money and it tempted me."

Brownmiller illustrates this idea of women as things, or property, by showing that in many cultures and among many men, when a married woman is raped, the view is held that *the husband* is the injured party—his property has been damaged. Or in the case of a virgin daughter, *the father*.

The circle of rape closes when the act is perpetrated by one man while another would further punish the object for "her" sin. Any law that would deprive a woman of freedom of choice and perpetuate the idea that she is property or a thing—whether it is the freedom to choose not to engage in sex or the freedom to choose not to give birth—is nothing short of legislative rape.

It fascinates me that I reacted to both Susan Brownmiller's book and Jerry Falwell's *Listen America!* with the same feeling of indignation. It is, of course, because both books really are about rape in that they deal with the premise of women as things who exist only for the purposes of men—be those purposes sex, targets for rage or contempt, or servitude. Jerry Falwell fully betrays his attitude when he cites this as a reason for his opposition to a piece of legislation related to the criminal code: "Women could sue their husbands for rape."

I am indignant that with the passage of the pending anti-choice legislation women's bodies—and henceforth our right to vote—will once again be up for grabs. But the other immediate consequences of this sort of legislation are such that even those who are opposed to abortion on moral grounds should pay close attention. Here are possible scenarios:

- You are forty-eight years old, and your doctor has told you that you can't get pregnant. It happens, however, that you become irregular, and you go in for a checkup and discover that the reason for your irregularity is not menopause but pregnancy. You know that having a baby at forty-nine means that you will be beyond retirement age when the child reaches adulthood. You also know that having a child this late poses a great risk that the child will be retarded or deformed. Sadly you tell your doctor you want an abortion. Just as sadly, he tells you that you can't have one.

  In contrast to the birth of your first child, the labor nearly kills you because of your age; and in contrast to your first child, who is now a delightful adult, the baby has a congenital heart problem, a cleft palate, and suffers from severe Down's syndrome.

  As the doctors spell out his various problems, you see clearly your life stretched before you with this child, who will require a great deal of surgery, a great deal of care, and who because of the degree of his retardation will remain little more than a vegetable.

- You have been told by your gynecologist that another birth could result in your death. Because of recent legislation prohibiting the use of the IUD, which worked well for you, you have switched to another, less effective form of birth control. You have just been told by your gynecologist that your new contraceptive has failed and you are now eight weeks pregnant. Well, unless you can afford to arrange a trip to Sweden or Japan, have underworld connections, or can locate a good back-alley butcher, you'd better make sure your Last Will and Testament is in order.

- A sixteen-year-old girl becomes pregnant after having intercourse just once. Unable to obtain help legally, she learns of a manicurist who does abortions on the side in a sleazy apartment over a liquor store. She and her boyfriend get together the required fee, and at the appointed time, lonely and afraid, she goes. There she is stretched out on a filthy kitchen table, and with no anesthetic, the product of her one transgression is brutally hacked at and yanked from her young body. Within days, after enduring excruciating pain, she bleeds to death. And what do you say about the beloved child you brought into the world and nurtured for sixteen years: "She made her bed; now she can lie in it"? Especially when that bed is a cold grave at an early age? Anyone who could say that, in my view, does not have the capacity for love required for good parenting.

- To her announcement that they're going to have a third child, her husband tells her, "Get an abortion." She is shocked when she learns that she can't, he is disbelieving. And even when he finally realizes the truth of the situation, he blames her for the contraceptive failure. The birth of the child turns out to be the straw that breaks the back of the marriage.

- She is thirty years old, married, and the mother of three children. She is in her own home, fully dressed, doing her housework. Her husband is at work, her kids are in school, and she has just come in from emptying the garbage, leaving the door slightly ajar. She returns to her chores and is surprised by a young man in his early twenties. Before she can speak or cry out, she becomes another victim, raped in broad daylight in her own home. Marital problems result when her husband can't get the idea of his wife being with another man out of his head. At just that point when he is coming to terms with his feelings, she learns she is pregnant, probably the result of the rape. Forced to watch his wife's pregnancy by another man progress, the old conflicts return with even greater force, and another marriage breaks down. Here is the family protected by the Moral Majority and Company.

- The woman is in her mid-twenties and already has three children. Overwhelmed by the responsibility of three, she believes a fourth will render her totally incompetent, if not totally mad. On learning that she is pregnant again, she becomes desperate. Not being "fortunate" enough to know of a manicurist who moonlights, she sticks a coat hanger up her vagina and bleeds to death on the floor of her bathroom. She is discovered by her three young children, who are now condemned to grow up without their mother.

- Conceived in rape, born in poverty, the boy has little chance for a decent life. Battered by his mother, he grows up with the ethic that you get what you want and debate the issues with violence. Delinquent at eleven, a street mugger at fourteen, he graduates to armed robbery when other kids his age are entering college. At twenty-one, with an arrest record as long as your arm, he breaks into a home in an upper-middle-class neighborhood, steals the silver, rapes the fourteen-year-old daughter, and murders her father when he responds to his child's cries for help. At twenty-two he is put to death in the gas chamber. His life begins and ends in full accord with ultraconservative principles.

- An eighteen-year-old woman becomes pregnant. She is not as yet ready for motherhood. Having been a battered child, raped by her father when she was just seven, beaten by her mother, she is too emotionally scarred to be a parent herself. She is unable to obtain a legal abortion, cannot find anyone to perform an illegal procedure, and she's just sensible enough not to try to do it herself. She has her baby, which, because it is the right thing to do, she keeps. Six months later the fetus so carefully protected by law is a statistic: the child has been battered to death.

III

THE BOTTOM LINE

Editor:

. . . Not since January 19, 1973, has the stock market closed at such a high plateau. The Dow Jones Industrial average again broke the thousand mark. Kindly note that Congress during this same period has finally taken up the question, "Does human life begin at conception?" After the Dow closed on that Friday (1/19/73), the following Monday, Black Monday, January 22, 1973, the Supreme Court handed down their infamous abortion decision. . . .

Letter-to-the-Editor
National Right-to-Life News
May 19, 1981

Doublespeak

It has long fascinated me that some of the pious see a connection between financial gain and the realization of what they perceive to be godly goals. Believing as I do that the truly spiritual or religious person would see virtue as its own reward and would often be characterized by a lack of interest in material wealth for himself or herself, this connection has seemed to me rather a contradiction. And it has confused me that Jerry Falwell and other Fundamentalist ministers show extreme confidence in preaching this contradiction: that materialism is a sin while capitalism, which I see as its primary source, is a virtue.

But more than anything else, opposition to abortion because of a "reverence for life" is irreconcilable with the movement's seeming indifference to a fetus once it becomes a real living, breathing baby. Rational and kind-hearted people support social welfare programs because they believe that no child should go to bed hungry or starve to death. These people support programs for the poor, for the old, and for the handicapped. Generally liberal, they are the people who would rather see their tax dollars used to improve the quality of life of all citizens than used for military purposes. It is very difficult for humanitarian people to accept the idea that those who are opposed to abortion on the grounds that it is the taking of a life are not similarly opposed to capital punishment or war. I cannot accept it and instead believe that the New Right that calls itself "pro-life" is truly *anti-life*.

How is one to reconcile these various aspects of the New Right agenda?

- A ban on abortion, even to save the life of a pregnant woman, based on a reverence for life

- Elimination of the welfare system, including lunches for poor schoolchildren, prenatal health care programs, and follow-up care for infants

- Stepping up military spending and sending American troops anywhere in the world to contain communism

- Capital punishment

- The right to bear arms

- No government interference in the personal lives of American citizens

To make their reverence-for-life points, the National Right-to-Life Committee compares abortion in the United States to Hitler's annihilation of six million Jews, calling it the American Holocaust. This is pretty fancy footwork. For one thing many of their fellow travelers insist that the Holocaust is a hoax and that any reference to it should therefore be deleted from our history books. Another problem with this argument is that when Hitler came into power, one of the first things he did was ban abortion and contraception because, according to his party-line doublespeak, birth control is "a violation of mother-hood." Another ploy the New Right uses is to compare themselves to the abolitionists. This is rather hilarious in view of the fact that, historically, white Fundamentalists have been the most racist members of our society—their opposition to busing today is a prime example. Leaders of the New Right may state that their position is based on a variety of other reasons that range from their objection to the government's interference in our private lives to their concern over lowered educational standards, but racism by any other name is still racism. Nothing so *enslaves* a woman—and for that matter, her husband and her family—as not being able to control her own fertility. And this is a problem that falls heavier on the poor woman, who just so often happens to be black.

The doublespeak of the New Right as pertains to reverence for life becomes clear with statistics: eighty-four percent of those who supported the Vietnam war are anti-choice, seventy-four percent of those who support capital punishment are anti-choice, and seventy-three percent of those who are anti-choice oppose handgun registration despite the fact that over ten thousand Americans are killed by handguns every year. On August 15, 1982, there appeared in the *San Francisco Sunday Examiner & Chronicle* an editorial cartoon that comes close to saying it all: A stout Senator is kneeling before a pregnant woman who is wearing a tattered dress, and he is saying, "Miracle of life." In the next frame, the woman, now unpregnant, wearing the same tattered dress, is standing with a tiny child at her knee and the good Senator is looking down upon her baby and saying, "Sniveling little welfare cheat."

When I pull together all of the various New Right positions, I see absolutely no reverence for life, let alone human dignity. In attempting to understand what such people mean by "reverence for life" and to reconcile all of their seemingly contradictory positions, however, I see that in a very perverse way they appear to be consistent.

As I explained in Chapter One, communism is seen by the New Right as Satan's plan in action, while capitalism is something that God bestowed on the United States at this country's inception. Thus anything whatsoever that can be construed as being anti-capitalistic is perceived as the work of the devil. There are no shades of gray. Social welfare systems, for example, are socialistic in nature, and are therefore based on communism, and hence are Satanic in nature.

This also explains the seeming contradiction in the New Right's reaching out to the common or working man while standing in opposition to labor unions. Labor unions, according to Jerry Falwell, have destroyed the capitalist work ethic by obtaining for the worker automatic pay increases and fringe benefits, thus reducing incentive. Labor unions are tools of Satan.

It may also seem to be a contradiction that the New Right decries government interference with the personal lives of Americans on the one hand, while on the other it advocates a ban on abortion and certain forms of birth control that puts the government into the most private of all personal sectors—the bedroom. According to pure Fundamentalist thought, however, there is no contradiction. The New Right objection to the government relates only to a particular form of government—the one based on the ethic of separation of church and state and on the freedom of all of the citizens of this country to practice the religion of their choice. We have lived with the democratic adaptation of that principle for so long that we tend to believe that what we know is how it has always been.

As John H. Redekop explains it so well in *The American Far Right* (1968), Fundamentalists have always believed in separation of church and state and the freedom to practice religion. The basic difference between their belief in this ethic and the average American's is that they base their belief on the fact that when this nation was founded, our forebears were concerned about religious persecution and so wrote into our Constitution that the state could not ban or interfere with the practice of a particular religion, but they see no problem the other way around. At the same time, while Fundamentalists are absolutely militant about the freedom to practice religion, they do not mean just any religion: they mean the freedom to practice Protestant Fundamentalism.

A component of their belief system is that *secular* government should not be able to interfere in the personal lives of the citizens, but a government based on Fundamentalism not only should be able, but has an obligation, to set down rules of conduct that are carved into legislative stone. In other words any law that can be construed as biblically ordained, even though it may come from a still imperfect secular government, is acceptable. The bottom line is that the far right mentality does not want interference from a government that it collectively perceives as being secular, but does want it if the government is one that follows its own Fundamentalist blueprint.

To understand fully what appears to be not just a contradiction but madness, it must be understood that they say what they truly do mean: the *stated* goal of the Moral Majority, which *does* speak for all of the splinter groups, is to turn our nation into what they think it was in the beginning—a biblical, Christian nation.

The Hidden Agenda

If wealth, the product of capitalism, is seen as a gift from God for doing good, the acquisition of it is seen as doing God's work.

The perpetuation of the patriarchy, the procreation ethic, the issue of freedom of choice—this whole package is good for the economy of the nation. The family—"the basic unit"—you will recall from Chapter One, is not revered because of the people who comprise it, but because the "unit" as such is the glue that holds God's capitalism together.

Thus patriarchy must prevail. As I said earlier, the feminine mystique turned women into baby-makers and thing-buyers, seemingly intent only on aggrandizing their homes and looking feminine. The fact that this created unprecedented prosperity was lost on no one. Including, I am certain, members of the far right community as well as the Fortune 500. As Landon Y. Jones put it in his book *Great Expectations* (1980):

> As the economic and baby booms surged on together, the cheerleading became almost feverish. Public-service signs went up in New York City subways reading, "Your future is great in growing America. Every day 11,000 babies are born in America. This means new business, new jobs, new opportunities." After-dinner speakers began to talk about "Prosperity by Population" and lofted tantalizing guesses of up to five million new babies a year by 1975. Financial magazines editorialized about the joys of "this remarkable boom." "Gone, for the first time in history," announced *Time* in 1955, "is the worry over whether a society can produce enough goods to take

care of its people. The lingering worry is whether it will have enough people to consume the goods."

The most euphoric article of all, perhaps, was a story *Life* printed in 1958, at the height of the boom. Three dozen children were crowded onto the cover along with the banner headline: KIDS: BUILT-IN RECESSION CURE—HOW 5,000,000 A YEAR MAKE MILLIONS IN BUSINESS. Inside the article began with another headline—ROCKETING BIRTHS: BUSINESS BONANZA—and continued chockablock with statistics and photographs about new citizens who were "a brand-new market for food, clothing, and shelter. . . ." A rhapsodic *Life* clinched its case by visiting Joe Powers, a thirty-five-year-old salesman from Port Washington, New York. He and his wife, Carol, had produced ten children and were buying 77 quarts of milk and 28 loaves of bread a week, just for starters. Faced with examples like that of meritorious devotion to the Procreation Ethic, little wonder that some American mothers felt as if it were their *duty* to have children. . . .

Then the baby boom peaked, and in 1964 people started having fewer children. And when the first baby-boomers themselves began to move into their childbearing years, the late sixties and seventies happened, bringing an emphasis on freedom of choice, a questioning of the procreation ethic, options beyond mothering for women, and a genuine concern about what overpopulation was doing to the environment, all followed by the quest for personal fulfillment. The result, as we know, is that increasing numbers of people have been delaying parenthood, opting for the small family, and a small number has even been opting for not having any children at all.

What a revolting development this must be for American business! Corporations that had been making money hand over fist no doubt had expected the boom to go on forever. Then along came the women's movement and the consequent baby bust, causing patriotic businessmen to regroup and fight back for the Yankee dollar.

Although the business community and the mass media have never really eased up on the baby-sell, in the early seventies I noticed a few changes. There were made-for-TV movies such as *Goodbye, I Love You* and *Tell Me Where It Hurts*—films that reflected the changes that were taking place for American women. And then, of course,

Norman Lear gave us *Maude,* liberated Gloria in *All in the Family,* and liberated Ann, a divorced mother, in *One Day at a Time.* Even some of the commercials were starting to take on a different flavor for a while: There were men doing laundry every now and then instead of simply telling women how to do it; marine biologists who were also mothers; a shampoo commercial featuring a re-entry woman saying, "I've got a new job, a new life, and I feel great."

But all that seems to have changed. The TV networks have gradually eased off the air any programs with a modicum of social significance, culminating with a near clean sweep by 1983 with the demise of such shows as *Lou Grant, M*A*S*H, Barney Miller,* and *WKRP,* all of which weren't simply first-rate shows but shows that, coincidentally, *never* focused on stereotypical family life and would never persuade people to try to emulate the offered parental model, as the prime-time shows of the fifties and sixties did.

Once again pregnancy and motherhood scream out at us from the covers of magazines, whether it is Princess Diana's or the more ordinary pregnancies of career women who have delayed motherhood. A flood of articles in newspapers and magazines speaks to the joys of motherhood after thirty, along with articles that warn women that they'd better think twice about waiting too long. And then, of course, there is a lot of hype about natural childbirth being a "peak experience," something not to be missed—seemingly whether or not one is interested in becoming a parent for the eighteen years following the experience. It is also a peak experience for fathers who, as we know, participate and bring their Nikons along to record the event for posterity. While much of the general hype seems to be aimed at women, there has been a rash of articles that talk about the joys of older fatherhood and having second families—presumably after trading in the old nag for a younger brood mare.

And along with Princess Diana, celebrity pregnancy is in once again, with media attention being focused on Faye Dunaway, Jaclyn Smith, Sissy Spacek, Donna Summer, Ursula Andress, and Jill Clayburgh—whose nude pregnant body was recently photographed for *Vogue*—and their glorious pregnancies, wonderful births, and joys as new, older mothers. It is what columnist Beverly Stephen calls "pregnancy chic," and it entices ordinary women to follow the example despite the fact that their mothering experiences could never match those of wealthy celebrities who can hire nannies to take care of their babies while they resume their glamorous careers without ever having to get up for the 2:00 A.M. feeding.

But apparently it doesn't work on a lot of people. While there will always exist people who buy myths, today many more are aware and have grown accustomed to their options. And while feminism and awareness of the negative effects of overpopulation may have played a role in convincing people to have smaller families, even women who would really prefer to be housewives are having fewer children because staying home is no longer an option for them.

When people have made up their minds on the matter, how do you persuade them to have more children? You don't. You *force* them.

Consider for a moment what might happen if the New Right were successful just in their bid to outlaw abortion and the use of IUD's and other forms of birth control that act as abortifacients. It is easy to predict that there would be many more unplanned pregnancies than usual, driving up the grand total of those women who would be predisposed to obtaining abortions. Would all of these women hop on airplanes and travel to Japan or Sweden? I rather doubt it. Those who did not use more desperate and dangerous methods would simply resign themselves and continue the pregnancy.

Not taking into account inflation, it is estimated that the cost of raising a child born today to adulthood will be anywhere between $147,000 and $247,000. The lion's share of that money will be spent on such things as diapers, clothing, food, shoes, furniture, tricycles, toys, bicycles, stereos, ski clothes, sporting goods, household products, and all of the hundreds and hundreds of commercially available things we middle-class parents feel our children must have. If just one million American women had one additional baby each year over a period of twenty years, the amount of money they would spend, mostly in goods, over the years it would take to raise them would be in the trillions. In fact, each year would set in motion the spending of trillions of dollars, one on top of each other.

From this point of view, the biblical edict to be fruitful and multiply becomes music in the ears of the capitalist Christian. And from this point of view it becomes easier to understand the marriage that exists between Christians and right-wing capitalists. For example, as reported in *Interchange,* Volume III, No. 4, August, 1981, Joseph Coors, owner of Coors Brewing Company, provided seed money that helped to found the conservative Washington "think tank" Heritage

Foundation, which is deeply intertwined with the Moral Majority. Other corporate financial supporters reportedly include Amway Corporation, the Dow Chemical Company, Motorola, and Sears, Roebuck and Co. Joseph Coors shows up again as having provided the seed money for the Committee for the Survival of a Free Congress, established for political action by Paul Weyrich (head of the Heritage Foundation); its goal is targeting pro-choice candidates for defeat.

Richard DeVos, Chairman of the National Association of Manufacturers, is reportedly involved with several Fundamentalist right-wing groups. He donated $25,000 to Christian Freedom Federation, a now defunct group that was organized to elect anti-choice conservative Christians to Congress. DeVos also happens to be a founding partner of Amway Corporation.

In their book *Danger on the Right* (1976), authors Arnold Forster and Benjamin R. Epstein report that "A total of 113 industrial, mercantile, and banking firms and twenty-five electric and gas companies have been identified as having contributed to organizations of the American right wing. This represents the *minimum* [emphasis mine] number of firms which have channeled significant amounts of funds into right wing causes."

Oil, steel, heavy machinery producers, and manufacturers of motors and motor controls, they say, tend to predominate. Some of the corporations listed as having contributed directly to such organizations or indirectly in the form of placing ads in New Right publications are: Allen-Bradley Corporation of Milwaukee; Technical Corporation of America; Eversharp, Inc.; the Republic and United Steel corporations; Gulf Oil; Humble Oil; Schick Safety Razor Company; Knott's Berry Farm; the Spindale and Cherokee Mills; the Flick-Reedy Corporation; Kenmetal, Inc.; the Henry Regnery Company; Dr. Ross Dog and Cat Food Company; and Hunt's Foods.

Individuals who have contributed to right-wing causes, the authors say, consist of a "group of approximately 250 men and women," a fair proportion of which are themselves the owners of business firms, corporation officials, corporate directors, and retired men of wealth. The more prominent names among them include Robert E. Wood, former Chairman of the Board of Sears, Roebuck and Co.; Roger Milliken, a textile manufacturer; and Harry Bradley of the Allen-Bradley Corporation.

The corporate mentality that has been responsible for polluting our environment and cheering on population growth is characterized by an obsession with profits. During the crash of 1929, for example, industrialists jumped to their deaths out of windows—their lives not being worth living without abundant wealth and power. Such an obsession is hard to reconcile with a "reverence for life." One is led to doubt that these various corporations would pump millions of dollars into the anti-choice movement because they collectively care about individual fetuses.

Births can be measured in dollars and cents. If the baby-boom children, born between 1946 and 1964, and all of those born since 1964 were forced to repeat the performance of the baby-boom parents—and then some—there would be an explosion of births the like of which is staggering to imagine. It would make the postwar baby boom look mild by comparison.

Can you imagine what that would do for business?

The Poor Pay More

Initially I had thought that stripping poor women of their reproductive rights was simply a first step toward the goal of stripping middle-class consumers of those rights. But the business community may also derive benefits from the procreation of the poor. Many years ago I saw a PBS documentary, *The Poor Pay More*. Its thesis was that poor people paid more for inferior merchandise because, while it was cheaper than quality merchandise, it was overpriced. Often, it was pointed out, poor people bought this inferior merchandise on the installment plan, paying exorbitant interest rates. It was then shown that the merchandise, especially furniture, would give out long before it was paid for; then those who had bought it just replaced it with more inferior merchandise, locking themselves into a cycle of indebtedness for the rest of their lives.

This cycle raises the possibility that even though archconservatives would like to see the social welfare system disappear, there may be a corporate benefit in its existence. So, as long as it does exist, merchandisers can skim off some cream for themselves. And it is pretty well acknowledged that the middle class, and not the superrich or the corporations, are the ones who pick up the tab for the welfare program. It could even be speculated at this point that while true believers would like to see the welfare system disappear because it is the work of the devil, fiscal conservatives who are not religious fanatics might not like to see it disappear at all, although they advocate its abolishment as a device to reach the middle-class worker who is sick and tired of paying the lion's share of income taxes. Identifying the poor as the source of the worker's high taxation does deflect heat from those corporations and the superrich who pay little or no income taxes and diverts attention from the fact that the middle classes are stuck with high taxes because the bulk of the national budget is being pumped into the arms build-up.

In any event, a marriage has obviously been made between fanatical religious groups and certain businessmen who finance them, leading them to support identical causes for, perhaps, different reasons. I say perhaps because while *some* New Right religious leaders, and probably *most* who follow them blindly, are sincere, I have serious doubts about people like Jerry Falwell, whose bottom line, I do believe, is measured by power and wealth.

The Kingdom, the Power, and the Glory

> For thine is the kingdom, and the power, and
> the glory, forever . . .

To say it was beautiful. To sing it exquisite. I grew up with it and it meant to me a loving God—and a God I love. It would, however, require a miracle for me to believe that it means the same thing to Jerry Falwell, whose religious fervor, I am convinced, is directed to "the Kingdom, the Power, and the Glory" in terms of Gold.

One week I turn on *The Old Time Gospel Hour,* and Mr. Falwell has announced his "Save a Baby Campaign." Declaring 1982 to be "The Year of the Unborn Child," he tells his audience that he's going to erect a monument similar to that of "The Tomb of the Unknown Soldier" and call it "The Tomb of the Unborn Child." He's going to, he says, launch a campaign to offer an alternative to abortion to pregnant teenagers, putting posters in phone booths and restrooms asking "Pregnant? Need Help?" and listing a number to call. When these girls call, they will be brought first to Jesus and next to a good Christian home to be cared for during pregnancy. When their babies are born, they will be adopted by good Christian couples. But all of this *costs,* he emphasizes over and over, so "Please send as large a gift as possible."

The kingdom, the power, the glory, and the money.

The following week he adds to his plea for Christian charity a healthy dose of guilt. It seems that he has learned that the United Way makes grants to godless Planned Parenthood "abortion mills" (never mind that abortion is not Planned Parenthood's major activity), so if you've been contributing to the United Way, you've been sinning. But you know how you can redeem yourself: Send your dollars to him. And while he lays on the guilt he also manages to undercut United Way. I would imagine that one goal is to have the faithful stop contributing to United Way (as millions of people do through payroll deductions) and send those contributions instead to his campaign. That he can be so transparent tells you something about what he thinks of the mentality of his followers. Evidently he subscribes to P. T. Barnum's maxim that a sucker is born every minute.

The kingdom, the power, the glory, and the money.

After trying to cut United Way out of some of the action, he launches his campaign to save starving Haitian children (what about starving American children?). Just $45 will feed one of these poor starving children for a year. Search your heart, your conscience, and your pocketbook. Give till it hurts. But resist allowing your tax dollars to help a needy American.

The kingdom, the power, the glory, and the money.

The following week he launches his save *The Old Time Gospel Hour* campaign. He tells us that he needs five thousand people to give $1,000 each to raise the one million needed to keep the show from being dropped by many stations. The fact that five thousand times one thousand happens to equal five million again tells you something about his opinion of the audience.

The kingdom, the power, the glory, and the money.

When he's not saving, he's peddling: his books, Bibles, tapes, lapel pins (one is a replica of the feet of a ten-week fetus, called "Precious Feet"), and all manner of paraphernalia each and every week. And each and every week, according to journalist Chuck Fager ("Falwell and Co.—On the Skids or Speeding Up?", *In These Times, San Francisco Chronicle,* May 5–11, 1982), alternating between the Moral

Majority and *The Old Time Gospel Hour,* he sends out desperate appeals to his followers. In *Thunder on the Right* (1980) Alan Crawford tells us that each and every week *The Old Time Gospel Hour* rakes in over one million dollars.

The kingdom, the power, the glory, and the money.

One of Falwell's more innovative direct-mail solicitations came about in June of 1982, when vandals cut down the antenna tower of his radio station. In a letter to the faithful that began with the word "Sabotage?" he wrote that replacing the tower for WRVL "is going to cost thousands and thousands of dollars. And being off the air these many days is very costly. So I'm turning to you now to ask if you can send a special gift of $100 immediately to get us back on the air." In a postscript Falwell added, "Let's defeat the devil and get back on the air in the next few days."

"But he left out one detail," writes Paul A. Engelmayer (*The Wall Street Journal,* July 6, 1982): "WRVL's damage is covered by insurance." Engelmayer's source is a claims representative, Paul Harris, of Home Insurance Company of Roanoke, Virginia, who said that the policy will pay all damages and equipment costs. It could be said that Falwell, busy man that he is, was unsure of this coverage. However, Engelmayer says that "When asked, Mr. Falwell acknowledges that he expects the insurance to cover 'whatever was destroyed in the incident.' "

The kingdom, the power, the glory, and the money.

What sort of person responds to these desperate appeals that electronic preachers like Falwell make? A woman I know is a divorced mother of two children. She works as a secretary and receives a small amount of child support for her two children, so she must carefully budget her money. She allows an expenditure of $35 each month for each child's clothing and other incidentals. On a guilt-ridden impulse, according to her teenage daughter, she wrote a check for $100 and sent it off. The young woman told me, "That represents what she planned to spend on me for three months." While it could be said that such a woman is irresponsible and foolish, what is more important to me is that people like Falwell tap into the needs and the guilt of those who are vulnerable and exploit their faith and trust.

Falwell and his fellow Fundamentalists are far from alone in such exploitations. The Mormon Church does it, but does it a bit differently. In the name of God, of course, the church demands a tithe from its member families. According to Mary Kay Allen, a former Mormon, although the Mormon Church frowns on women working outside the home, many Utah women do so—because that's the only way the family can afford to pay the tithe. As she put it to me: "These women take menial or part-time jobs and leave their children unsupervised just so they can earn the money to pay the tithe."

The bottom line.

The hell with the kingdom and the glory. Let's hear it for the power and the money.

Inequality as Another Bottom Line

Not only do corporations have a vested interest in procreation simply because more babies means the buying of more things, it is also in their interests to defeat any legislation that would serve the cause of equality. Thus anti-choice legislation, which helps to serve this cause as well as the economic one, is but part of a package that, in my view, is designed to keep women in their lowly places. As pointed out by Walda Katz Fishman and Georgia Fuller in "Unraveling the Right-Wing Opposition to Women's Equality" (1981), there exists a distinct economic advantage to corporations maintaining inequality.

> The major backers of the right wing are and always have been corporations. Corporations are in the business for profits, not for people. Women have historically been a low-paid, marginal labor pool. Today, working women earn only 59¢ for every $1.00 earned by working men. This means that if a husband and wife both work, that family is, on the average, putting two workers into the labor force at a cost to industry of about one and a half.
>
> . . . It is "good business" to pay women less, to pay minorities less, to keep workers from organizing.

In this light it could easily be concluded that the ultra-right position that holds that labor unions are agents of Satan and communism is just a handy cover story for opposition on economic grounds. To understand all of this, Fishman and Fuller say, distinctions must be made between the political leadership and the financial backers and the grassroots followers:

> Right-wing leaders have a clear understanding of what they are doing and why. They are protecting big business—its profits, power and privileges. They cannot, however, overtly propose this agenda. . . .

They correctly point out that the use of such appeals as "traditional family," and "old-time religion" are central to the exploitation of women's issues and mask the genuine, hidden agenda of the New Right.

There is no reason to believe that part of that agenda does not include a ban on *all* forms of birth control. The Catholic hierarchy, remember, is just as opposed to "unnatural" birth control as it is to abortion. The American Life Lobby has taken a position opposing all forms of birth control, and most pro-life people I've talked to over the years are similarly opposed. And certainly fiscal conservatives, eager for another baby boom, could be counted on for support.

It may seem far-fetched, especially to those who take access to birth control for granted, but should the New Right ever gain that slight edge of control they need in our Congress, we can kiss that option good-bye.

And were that to come to pass, the catch-22 that women are currently living with would certainly tighten. Having children already virtually guarantees that a woman will need to work. The more children she has, the more locked into working outside the home she will be. With more children, more work, more financial need, and more overwhelmed than ever, she is the perfect candidate for collapse or child neglect.

IV

WEEP FOR THE CHILDREN

It is paradoxical to us that the same leaders who are currently demanding that women bring their babies to term are simultaneously voting to cut off food stamps, child nutrition programs, and related benefits essential for the health of our children.

The National Coalition of
American Nuns
May 1982

The last few weeks have been tough for some kids. A newborn baby was dumped into bushes on Noriega Street in San Francisco. A baby girl swaddled in newspapers was put out with the trash in the Mission District. . . . A newborn girl was found dead in a front yard on 25th Street. . . .

Scott Winokur
San Francisco Sunday Examiner & Chronicle
May 28, 1982

. . . For the purposes of this Act, the term "child abuse and neglect" does not include discipline or corporal punishment methods applied by a parent or individual explicitly authorized by a parent to perform such function.

Excerpted from
The Family Protection Act

God-given Rights?

It did not surprise me to open my newspaper approximately one year after reading that our Congress had voted to restrict abortion for poor women and learn that the abandonment of infants had become nearly epidemic. Given the current administration's determination to save you and me—and Exxon, of course—a tax dollar here and there, it was not hard to predict. And I expect it to get worse. As Cathy Baxter, executive director of San Francisco's Child Abuse Council, told reporter Scott Winokur, "We'll see an increase in abandonments when parents really start feeling the cutbacks in Aid to Families with Dependent Children, nutritional programs, and food stamps."

As poor women become pregnant, and Senator Helms's legislation keeps them from exercising their Constitutional right to choose, we will see history repeating itself. Before the Supreme Court wiped all restrictive abortion laws off the books, infants were frequently tossed into garbage cans or tossed out in brown paper bags in parks.

More frightening even than this barbarism is the number of unwanted children who will be less mercifully dealt with and who will become part of the statistics that tell us that some two million children are physically abused annually in the United States. According to Dr. Vincent Fontana, a pediatrician, one of the nation's leading authorities on child abuse, and author of the book *Somewhere a Child Is Crying,* child abuse is already the number one killer of children in this country. More children, he says, die at the hands of their parents or other caretakers than as a result of any "childhood disease," including leukemia and muscular dystrophy.

With child abuse as epidemic as it is, this tragic social problem is strangely absent from the Religious New Right's litany of all that is wrong with the family and society. For all of their talk about crime, for example, and their indictment of permissiveness, feminism, television, and pornography as root causes, I have never once heard any member of the Religious New Right make reference to the fact that *100 percent of the inmates in San Quentin were battered when they were children* (Crawford, 1980).

One would think that law-and-order types that they are, they would jump on top of this statistic. And certainly, moralists that they are, one would also think that they would hold the abuse of children as most sinful. Yet they appear to hold precisely the opposite view, and, in fact, the programs and policies they advocate are just the sort that, if realized, would give license to parents who think there's nothing wrong with battering a child. One example is the aforementioned excerpt from the Family Protection Act. For another example, in the fall of 1980 the Moral Majority was responsible for the defeat of the Domestic Violence Prevention Act, which would have allocated $56 million to help fund shelters for battered women and children. In South Carolina they've been helping a father regain custody of his son —taken away because of severe abuse—and in Indiana they've been lobbying for repeal of all child abuse laws on the grounds that they interfere with the right of a parent to "discipline" his child. Their ultimate goal seems to be to restore full authority to parents. They regard children as the property of their parents, who should thus be able to do with them whatever they choose.

A good example of right-wing thought as pertains to the guidance of children was published in the 1982 issue of *Forerunner*. In an article entitled "Who Is Raising Our Children?", Richard Fugate tells us that:

> Because of God-granted parental authority, parents have the right to set their will above that of their children and to command them to follow their rulership. They also have the power to administer justice and to punish for disobedience or to rear for conformance to their commands.

Citing Colossians 3:20, Fugate goes on to say that children must obey their parents in all things, they must do whatever they are told to do: they must never question authority. ("Johnny, I told you to kill the cat; now kill the cat.")

> Neither society, school personnel, nosy individuals, not even other institutions have any authority over children. The parents' power over their children is accountable to government only through God's laws. . . . The child has only the God-given right to be raised by his parents without the intervention of any other institution.

But, he laments, currently parental authority is being undermined through child advocacy agencies and child abuse laws. "Parents," he says, "must not allow government to usurp their authority in those areas in which God holds the parents alone accountable."

Under the heading "God's Protection of Parental Authority by Government," he then cites Matthew 15:4: "For God commanded, saying Honor thy father and mother: and, He that curseth father or mother, let him die the death," and Exodus 21:15: "And he that smiteth his father, or his mother, shall be surely put to death."

When we see a child receive what we consider mistreatment from a parent, this obscenity continues, "we must remember that God is in control and has chosen to place the soul life of that child under those parents specifically."

The idea that children are the property of parents who have unquestioned authority over them is, significantly, one that is commonly held by battering parents, who use "discipline" as their excuse for violence. Quite different from those overwhelmed parents who find themselves on the brink of situational abuse (this will be discussed later), these are parents who do not think there's anything wrong with abusing *their* children. In *Somewhere a Child Is Crying* (1973), Dr. Vincent Fontana has this to say of the "disciplinarian":

> Disciplinarians may have mixed motives, but their rationale for speaking roughly to their little boy and beating him when he sneezes is the age-old one that to spare the rod is to spoil the child. . . . They are likely to explain their punitive actions by saying that this is the way they were brought up and this is the way they intend to bring up their children. And they *were* brought up that way, beaten themselves and taught to believe in the fist and the stick as necessary means of discipline. Superficially, they are only living out our national belief that physical punishment is a legitimate method of child rearing. Possibly the most effective way of compelling obedience. If "normal" disciplinary practices include slaps, ear-tuggings and energetic spankings, how easy it is to justify severe beatings or chaining a child to a bedpost. "It's for his own good. How else will he ever learn to do as he is told?"

The adult who is reproached for this behavior is astonished or appears to be. First, it is his right to bring up his child as he pleases. Second, he is only trying to do the very best he can to "teach respect," "straighten the kid out," "wallop the nonsense out of him," make him grow up to be "a useful citizen." These individuals claim not to understand why severe physical punishment is not acceptable or effective. What was right for their parents was right for them. After all, look how well *they* turned out. In many cases, these are rigid people who do not consciously believe that they are doing anything wrong. Even if the punishment, which they tend to carry to extremes, results in the permanent maiming or death of the child, they may still see themselves as in the right. . . .

. . . [T]he disciplinarian-parent frequently couples an I-am-God attitude with a terrible anger or a ferocious pleasure in what he is doing. In his own way, he, like other abusers, is striking out against the child in anger and frustration, secure (if falsely) in the knowledge that corporal punishment is part of the American way.

Sexual Child Abuse and the Authoritarian Family

Something else that may well be "part of the American way" is the sexual abuse of children. The estimates range from one female in a hundred to one in three who will have been sexually abused before she reaches adulthood. It depends on who you talk to and what you read, but my sources at Parents Anonymous say it is closer to one out of three. My experience on a parental stress hot line bears this out. Although it is still a fairly taboo subject, which makes the reporting of it scant, it seems that I'm constantly having someone—older women I know, teenagers from good middle-class homes—tell me of their own experiences at the hands of their fathers. And Henry Giaretto, who founded the now national organization Parents United, the goal of which is to provide therapy for families in which incest has occurred, has told me, "What we're seeing now is just the tip of the iceberg. I think before we're through with this, we'll find out that sexual abuse is more prevalent than battering."

With their advocacy of total parental rule or ownership, the New Right plays right into the hands of the typical sexual abuser with still another of their advocacies: that sex education should be the exclusive purview of the parents. As Judith Lewis Herman, coauthor of *Father-Daughter Incest,* explains it:

> The idea of sex education seems to be anathema in highly traditional, devout, authoritarian, and male-dominated families —that is, in families where children are most at risk for sexual abuse. This should not be surprising, since incestuous fathers . . . have the most to lose if their children receive information from sources outside the family.
>
> . . . If an educational campaign for children and parents were carried out on a national scale, it would probably result in some degree of prevention. Some fathers might be discouraged from initiating an incestuous relationship if they could not assume that their wives and children were entirely naive. . . .
>
> But this reform alone can never be sufficient for the primary prevention of child sexual abuse. For the locus of the problem is ultimately in the structure of the family. As long as fathers rule but do not nurture, as long as mothers nurture but do not rule, the conditions favoring the development of father-daughter incest will prevail.

According to one report (*San Francisco Chronicle,* May 18, 1982), about sixty percent of all sexual child abusers are involved with adult partners, and many have children themselves. Dr. Gene G. Abel, director of the Sexual Behavior Clinic of the New York State Psychiatric Institute at Columbia-Presbyterian Medical Center in Manhattan, says that "some of these fellows are very rigid in their opinions of sexual morality—for example, they think it would be wrong to have an affair, and yet at the same time they might be having sex with their own children."

Sexual abuse usually starts when the victim is about eight years old (although incidents can occur any time between infancy and adolescence) and continues on into the teen years until the child leaves the family home—usually on the run—to escape. Typically the sexually abused teenage victim turns to drugs, alcohol, and promiscuous behavior. Long before that, however, she is told that she must never tell her mother because her mother won't love her anymore. Even though she is assured by her abusing father (or stepfather) that it is normal for a father and daughter to relate this way, somewhere along the line she learns otherwise and, typically, she feels immense guilt that completely destroys her self-esteem. Naturally she is reluctant to reveal her "badness" to anyone, so she doesn't seek help, and a child so abused bears the immense burden of knowing that if the secret is told, the family might fall apart—and that would be all her fault.

The prognosis for those who do not get competent professional help isn't good. I personally know a number of women who were sexually abused by their fathers or stepfathers, and all of them have said that they are able to lead normal lives now only as a result of intensive therapy over a period of many years. There is no precise way of knowing at this time how many women seek therapy to help them work through this particular trauma. Nor is there any way of knowing precisely how many promiscuous teenagers who take to the streets as prostitutes might have been sexual abuse victims. But we do know this: In a study of over two hundred street prostitutes, it was revealed that more than sixty percent of them had been sexually abused during their childhood and adolescence. The findings, compiled by Dr. Mimi H. Sibert and a team of psychologists and former prostitutes from the Delancey Street Foundation in 1982, also revealed that *two thirds of the women had come from middle-class, religious backgrounds.*

And then there is the physical damage that can be caused. In *The Best Kept Secret* (1980), Florence Rush reports on her in-depth research into this aspect of sexual abuse as follows:

> Adult sex with children presents an increasingly serious health problem. Cases of rectal fissures, lesions, poor sphincter control, lacerated vaginas, foreign bodies in the anus and vagina, perforated anal and vaginal walls, death by asphyxiation, chronic choking from gonorrheal tonsillitis, are almost always related to adult sexual contact with children. Of twenty cases of genital gonorrheal infection in children aged one to four, nineteen had a history of adult-child sex. A history of adult-child sex was obtained in all twenty-five cases of infected children between five and nine, and the same was true of all 116 cases of children between fourteen and fifteen. In another study, 160 of 161 cases of this illness in children resulted from sexual contacts with adults.

The patriarchal trap becomes quite complete for the young girl who, raped by her father, becomes pregnant and is forced to continue a pregnancy that is dangerous because of her age, and in any case, could ruin her life.

I am not suggesting that incest or child battering is practiced in every Fundamentalist Christian home. Rather, what I think must be exposed and examined is the manner in which seemingly unrelated mores, incidents, and facts may be more related than is obvious, and the very real danger that child abuse, sexual and otherwise, may be related to patriarchal attitudes. Such abuse can go undetected in an authoritarian society or subculture that places parents' rights above the rights of children to be protected. In *Against Our Will,* Susan Brownmiller writes:

> The unholy silence that shrouds the interfamily sexual abuse of children and prevents its realistic appraisal is rooted in the same patriarchal philosophy of sexual private property that shaped and determined the historic male attitude towards rape. For if a woman was man's corporal property, then children were and are a wholly owned subsidiary.

Speaking just to the "unholy silence," I would like to add that I have heard spokespersons for the New Right repeatedly express deep concern that schoolchildren are encouraged to share their family experiences and feelings with their classmates. The fear is that one of their children will reveal private matters that are "the business of the family only." I can honestly say that after seventeen years of parenthood, of all the things I worry about, my children talking about their home life is of such a low priority that it never made it onto my list of possible problems. This makes me wonder what in the world people so obsessed have to hide.

Violence in the Name of God

At some point you really have to wonder if some of the leaders of the Religious New Right, which is so intent on saving every fetus ever conceived while advocating attitudes and policies that foster child abuse, *hate* living children. A disturbing sign is that abusive practices are built into some of their schools. As reported by Michael Disend in the February 1982 issue of *Penthouse,* one Fundamentalist day-care center uses a makeshift electric chair as a disciplinary tool;

a pastor in Madison, Wisconsin, was charged with battery after he paddled a five-year-old child with an eighteen-inch redwood paddle; the principal of another Christian school in Durham, North Carolina, was charged with assault for hitting a six-year-old hyperactive child—whom he wouldn't allow to take his medication. And then there was a recent account that made coast-to-coast headlines when a Baptist pastor was found to be using a homemade electric stool and a six-volt battery to shock his young Bible students into hearing God's word.

One explanation for this sort of violence against children comes from the Reverend Greg Dixon, an electronic preacher, a member of the Board of Directors of the Moral Majority, and leader of a group in Indiana that lobbies to have that state's child-protection laws repealed. Dixon tells us that "people are born bad," and that "children are born sinners." And, he advises, "There's only one thing that can drive that out": biblical punishment according to God's law.

Taking this message further than any preacher might imagine is one man who freely admitted that he put his five-month-old baby girl on a heating grate that he called "the gateway to hell." The reason, as reported in the November 7, 1981, Associated Press account, for this father's action was to exorcise the demon within. The baby was, the father told investigators, actually the devil. The Deputy District Attorney in charge of the case told reporters, "It was like she was roasted," and explained that the heat of the grate had measured 200 degrees. The account goes on to report that this was not the only child this father had cooked. Convinced that the devil had taken possession of the body of his two-year-old son, he had also put this child on the grate. The boy survived, but had grate marks branded into the flesh of his buttocks and lower back. "I was casting out demons. I was trying to get them back to the fire of hell," he explained. "What I did was my way of showing how much faith I have in God." Prior to this double act of violence, this father had been constantly watching an evangelist on television. He believed, according to the account, that the Fundamentalist was talking directly to him when he preached that Armageddon would come soon.

In another case of alleged possession, a San Bernardino, California, couple watched their son die because they thought that his diabetes was caused by Satan and the insulin needed to treat it would strengthen the demons. According to a United Press International report on July 10, 1981, when the parents were put on trial for the death of their eleven-year-old son, their defense was that they were following the dictates of their Fundamentalist religion in refusing to give insulin to him. They thought he had been cured by a faith healer.

The boy had been under treatment for diabetes for some time, and was taking insulin when his parents took him to the First Assembly of God church. There, according to the report, a visiting faith healer performed a "laying on of hands" and pronounced the boy cured. Following this ceremony, the parents threw the boy's medication away, and when he started to go into insulin shock, his father saw it as a "lie of the devil." He told the authorities that he and his wife felt it would be a denial of God to give the child his medication and an invitation for the demon which had been cast out to return to the boy's body.

In the same article mentioned earlier, reporting the increase in child abandonment, Scott Winokur writes that a four-month-old baby was placed in the surf in an apparent ritual sacrifice and bobbed up and down in the water as his mother looked on. She told the police she had been ordered by Jesus to give the baby back to God. Chris Hatcher, who is Director of Family Therapy at the University of California's Langley Porter Psychiatric Institute in San Francisco, explained the case this way: "For some parents the child begins to have a ritualistic or symbolic kind of importance. Sacrifice is thought to result in a spiritual cleansing of the people involved or the child's soul." Another psychologist, Alicia Lieberman of the University of California's Infant–Parent Program said, "There are also mothers who feel that at particular times other people take over. These mothers hear 'voices' like God or the devil. These voices 'tell' them to do things. They might tell them to do something to the child."

These are extreme examples of religion having run amok, to be sure, but unfortunately they are not isolated cases. Many children have been hurt "in the name of God," by parents who thought they were exorcising demons, beating the badness out of their children, or offering them up as human sacrifices. More common, however, is the authoritarian parent who wants his or her child to be well behaved and will stop at virtually nothing to get the desired results. This parent punishes severely for all transgressions, whether large or small. While in training as a lay therapist to work on the parental stress hot line, I learned that the authoritarian abuser has unrealistic expectations of what a small child was actually capable of, expecting a three-year-old to understand and perform as well as a ten-year-old. We saw films that showed us severe beatings for bed-wetting, spilling milk, back-talk that in reality was only the predictable assertiveness of a "terrible two." There were cases wherein a child's wetting his pants cost him his life. As Dr. Vincent Fontana has observed, "I know there are people walking the streets who have murdered their own children."

The Hazards of Perfection

Situational child abuse is more preventable, but is more likely to be hidden from view. It is also likely to be exacerbated by policies of the New Right. Situational abuse occurs when a parent is under too much stress, has unrealistic expectations of the child, and of himself or herself—usually when there is a crisis. The mother who is likely to be a situational abuser is, first, ill-prepared for parenthood, one who is traditionally married and in the home all day with one or more young children and who strives for the perfection held out by the media and the feminine mystique. Given the reality of what being a full-time wife and mother in the home involves, she is unable to meet the artificial standards set for her, which causes her self-esteem to erode. Generally speaking this mother is both actually and psychologically isolated. Because she is so busy striving for perfection as a wife, homemaker, and mother while striving to rear perfect children, she cuts herself off from other adults. Such a parent worries to excess about how she looks to other people. She worries so much about what other people will think of her and her family that she may consider it a major crisis when her children do something that does not reflect well on her. And it is this worry about what the neighbors will think that makes it impossible for her to learn that she isn't the only mother in the world who isn't perfect.

She lives in a patriarchal pressure cooker with the very real demands of her children and her very unreal and unmet expectations. She is literally up against the wall, and when a crisis hits, she can't cope and is likely to lash out at a small child for even a trivial transgression—just being in the wrong place at the wrong time may be all that a child has to do.

One woman who called a parental-stress hot line told of an experience that is sadly typical:

> The day I threw the baby across the room was the day I'd just had it. Day in, day out, I tried to keep the house clean, keep the three-year-old out of mischief, read to the four-year-old, get the laundry done. The baby had been crying all day, the dog shit on the rug, and then toward afternoon when the house was still a mess, the washing machine gave out. It was just after the bank called to tell me I was overdrawn on my account that I simply went berserk. I picked up the baby, who had been ravaging my nerves, and threw him.

To learn the effect of this striving for traditional perfection, one has only to go to Utah, home of the perfect patriarchy. The model that the Religious New Right would like to impose on all of us can be seen in Mormonism, which keeps women chained in subserviency and espouses the joys of parenthood in exaggerated form.

As is well known, the Mormon Church emphasizes large families. Mothers are likely to be under stress in direct proportion to how many children they might have. And while this state where children are supposed to bring joy is only the thirty-fourth most populous state, it ranks thirteenth in per-capita reported cases of child abuse (Associated Press, June 27, 1982). As one Salt Lake City social worker, Jane Bebb, put it, "By virtue of being a parent, every one of us has the potential to abuse. It doesn't matter what the religion, but when you have a heavy load of shoulds, don'ts, dos, some people just aren't going to make it." Those who live under Mormon dictates, or under the feminine mystique, carry around an unbearable load of shoulds.

To find out more about what is happening in Utah I spoke to a woman there who has been taking care of children whose overwhelmed mothers have abandoned them. When I asked her what she thought was causing this outbreak of abuse and neglect, she said that strict adherence to church doctrine and the patriarchy has created a situation wherein mothers believe that they have to be absolutely perfect, that they have to do everything themselves, with no help from their husbands:

One mother whom I never would have expected to fall apart was absolutely perfect. Her children were fashion plates, her house spotless, and she catered to her husband. She was from England but had come here when she was very young. She was very, very proper, very devout, and the perfect Mormon wife. One day she simply up and went back to England, leaving her children behind.

Typically the women who abandon their families have too many children and all the responsibility, and one day they just say to their husbands, "Look, I've done it all these years, now it's your turn." The men, with no knowledge whatever of child care, frequently wind up neglecting or abusing the children.

And the women who batter are those who don't cut and run but those who just blow sky-high from all the pressure to be perfect and to have perfect children to show to the world.

"Child abuse of all types," she told me, "is rampant. On top of everything else," she explained, "Mormons isolate themselves from anyone but their immediate families and their wards." Incest, she said, is commonplace. "Despite all of the pious preachings, Mormon attitudes practically *breed* incest, and many Mormon families have no moral standards whatever." She said there exists incest between fathers and daughters, stepfathers and stepdaughters, and between brothers and sisters. "The reason for this incest in the children, I think, is that these kids are shown very little affection, and often boys and girls share the same bedroom in big families—so, craving love, they turn to each other."

When I asked her if there were any hot lines or other organized efforts to intervene and help potentially abusive parents, she explained that there were probably more such services in Utah than in most other states. "We have hot lines, and we have drop-in child-care centers where people can leave their kids to keep from beating them up, but they go largely unused, and abuse continues behind closed doors.

"Mormons, possibly more than anyone else on the face of the earth—with the exception of conservative Fundamentalists who are totally consumed with their churches—are obsessed with what other people will think of them." Apparently, rather than have anyone think they have the same potential to abuse as everyone else, or problems they can't cope with, these image-conscious people would, perversely, continue to mistreat their children.

The woman I spoke to is angry. She wants to help the children, but is at a loss as to what to do. She feels betrayed. Her ancestors came to Utah with Brigham Young, so her roots in Mormonism run as deep as is possible. But she emphatically blames the dogma and the demands of the church and the present leadership that so oppresses women for the child abuse and for, until recently, sweeping it under the rug. The Mormon Church, she says, is a closed community that cuts itself off from outside efforts or ideas in order to correct social ills. Her last words to me were "My husband and I have *asked* to be excommunicated from the church. I don't want my name on their rolls. I don't want anything whatever to do with those people."

About two months after this conversation, I received the following letter from Mary Kay Allen, who lives in West Jordan, Utah:

Utah's state emblem is the beehive. This is interesting when you stop and ask yourself what does a state emblem represent? In Utah, our emblem is supposed to represent the people, and in Utah, the majority of voters are Mormons. One need only give a small amount of thought as to the social order of a beehive. First of all there can be only one Queen Bee to a hive; the rest are only drones or workers. The latter are sentenced to toil their lives away for the benefit of the hive, realizing absolutely nothing for themselves independently from the hive. Isn't this not unlike the Latter-Day Saints, and for that matter many of the other conservative Christian churches?

How is it that these churches have such a stranglehold on their members? By brainwashing their victims at an early age, by manipulation through family and friends, by social discrimination, and the list goes on and on.

Here in Utah most folks feel that to be religious you must be a member in good standing of the Mormon Church. Don't ever mention that religion and church are not synonymous. Some of these Mormons might have a fit of apoplexy. Of course, this attitude contributes to some pretty harsh social pressures calling for their followers to attend church functions *religiously,* tithe (to the tune of ten percent of everything they make), have as many kids as possible, get married in the Temple, send their kids on mission, accept any and all appointments by the bishop, and study the books of Mormon, Doctor and Covenants, and the Pearl of Great Price. (Of course, with everything else they have to do, there isn't much time for studying.) This is a bonus for the Church, because the less their members really know, odds are the Church will be able to keep them kowtowing longer.

What effect does this have on the people as a whole? Well, a lot of these people are understandably tired and drained; they are broke from shelling out tithing, buying shoes, clothing, and other necessities to attend church functions (one would be looked down upon by their peers if not dressed just so). Their nerves are frayed, and most of the time there are a lot of brats underfoot.

Utah is thirteenth in the nation for child abuse, we are right up there in the top of the national ratings for the size of families, and we are somewhere near the top for having so many teenage mothers. Yet we are pretty near the bottom in the nation economically. Roll all this into a ball and you can see why it is our kids are getting abused.

The contributing factors to the increase of child abuse are social pressures, financial problems, and improper priorities. Stresses such as these on our personal lives are causing more and more parents to lash out at their children.

It is in times like these that people should be able to turn to their religions for the solace they so badly need, not to a church or synagogue, but to the Lord.

When a troubled mother finally gets to the breaking point from trying to meet others' expectations, she is supposed to turn to the bishop of her ward for guidance. Most bishops have no background whatever to draw upon to be capable of counseling these women. Their experience does not enable them to understand a feeling of complete loneliness and uselessness. Is it any wonder that so many women are deserting their families? Every Mormon woman I have talked to who has taken this route has told me, "I just couldn't live that way anymore." But why, you ask, would they leave their children? Because they come from a predominantly Mormon background. Their parents are Mormons, their friends are Mormons, everybody is Mormon. These women know that they would get very little support from family or friends. After all, they had perfectly good Mormon husbands (who probably behaved according to the philosophy that the way to keep a woman is to keep her knocked up and barefoot). They had their church work, their children, their houses—why, they had everything. Everything, that is, except their own identity. They've tried to be what the church, their parents, their husbands, their children, their neighbors, and their friends expected them to be. In short, they've put their faith in man and been sorely disappointed.

Prevention Through Planning

Child abuse is a very complicated phenomenon that cuts across all socioeconomic and ethnic lines. Its prevention depends on breaking cycles that are currently in force in American families, and this can only be accomplished through a recognition of the problem and through the continuation of those organizations that have been established to help the battering parent and the battered child: Families Anonymous, Parents Anonymous, social service programs, and the hundreds of other hot-line groups and centers that have sprung up across the nation. Prevention is also largely dependent upon keeping cycles of abuse from getting started in new generations where previously no abuse has existed, and the very best way to accomplish this is through family planning. I define family planning as: being fully aware of what's involved in the parental role, having realistic expectations of oneself as a parent and of small children, having the capacity to assess one's potential skills as a parent, and being aware of any conflicts that may ultimately place a child in jeopardy. *And having full access to all forms of birth control, including abortion.* When people plan anything, or do it intentionally, they have an expectation that the outcome will be positive. Unfortunately, underneath the desire in many people to have children lies the fundamental belief in the motherhood myths that were spawned by the idiotic feminine mystique, which holds that parenthood is always wonderful and easy, and which continues to pressure women to have children to conform to social norms.

The mystique bore little resemblance to real life, as we know, and it essentially prepared (and continues to prepare) people for the parental role by informing them that all children are cute, sweet, funny, and lovable; none ever cry, get dirty, make messes, or fling themselves on the floor of the supermarket while kicking and screaming. Mothers are beautiful, fathers are handsome, and everyone lives happily ever after in houses that are always elegant and clean.

In 1971 I started interviewing women who had bought all the myths, and I haven't stopped. Nor have I stopped getting mail from them. To this day I receive letters from women who believed it all only last year. And what these women have revealed to me over the years is that, at some level of consciousness, they had children because they were pressured into doing so. Some say they now realize that they only thought they wanted to have children, while others say they had them because "it was the thing to do." And those who adopted because they could not have biological children were no exception. Their planned children were the result of social pressure of some sort and were wanted not for themselves but instead desired as symbols of normalcy or conformity—or because it would all be oceans of fun.

Added to the social pressure that still exists to have children is a component of the feminine mystique most commonly found in conservative churches: the infantalization of females. Put that together with pressure to have children, unrealistic expectations, which we can thank the media for perpetuating, virtually no preparation for this important responsibility, and you have a blueprint for situational child abuse.

And if adult married homemakers have difficulty reconciling myth with reality and coping with the stresses of parenthood, consider the teenage mother. Some teenagers "plan" to have children because they want something of their own and someone to love them, or think it would be "cool" to have a baby. Over and over again the immature mother who batters her baby will explain, "I wanted to have a baby to love me. When he cried all the time that proved he didn't love me, so I hit him."

According to an editorial in *The New York Times* on November 1, 1981, there is still another reason why teenagers intentionally have babies:

> . . . Why do so many young girls want babies? Doris McKelvy, whose Manhattan agency provides sex education,

counseling and adoption services, offers the prevailing professional view. Many young girls in the central city live in such neglect and hopelessness that they are desperate for attention and affection. They get pregnant, often "because they want to be babied themselves."

Yet often, joy and excitement rapidly give way to confusion, impatience and anger. Frequently the child is abused. . . .

In any event the connection between ignorance of motherhood, lack of planning, and child abuse is a clear one. Of the generation that brought it sharply into focus Landon Y. Jones (1980) has this to say:

. . . Child abuse—a classic sign that a family cannot cope—became most visible in the United States when the baby boom came to parenthood. The homicide rate for children aged 1–4 tripled between 1950 and 1975 and is now a greater cause of childhood mortality than any other disease. In the late 1970s, the age group that felt the largest percent increase in homicide was, sadly, 1–4. An estimated two million children are abused physically each year. . . .

It is a figure that bears repeating. *Two million children annually.*

More Doublespeak

The New Right plucks simple answers and tosses around statistics that mean nothing; and lost in the cracks are the real human facts. For instance, they cite as a reason for their concern over abortion the fact that the supply of newborn babies has dried up as a result of women having abortions. The tactics they are using to increase the supply are certainly less than ethical: they reach out to pregnant girls with the deceptive advertising of their "abortion counseling services," and once a scared pregnant girl takes the bait, their abortion counseling amounts to showing her gruesome pictures of aborted fetuses in an effort to persuade her to continue her pregnancy and place the baby for adoption. Deception in advertising is one name for this. If there exists a genuine concern that children be available for adoption, there is a large "supply" of older children, hungering for real homes but stashed in foster care and institutions. Why don't they market them?

We know the answer. They love only fetuses. They care not one whit about living children, nor one whit about living pregnant women. They manage to ignore every possible tragic ramification of their rigid position. It is of no interest to them, for example, that an unwanted pregnancy in an already stressful home can lead to such a severe degree of stress that it can render the environment dangerous to the children already in it. I have heard more than one distraught, depressed mother say that pregnancy at the wrong time was the trigger for abusing an already living child. As one woman put it:

> My marriage was a shambles, but I had hoped we could work things out. Part of our problem was that there was never enough money, and we fought about it all the time, with him accusing me of not being a good manager. Hell, there wasn't all that much to manage. Needless to say, there wasn't any money left over so I could hire a sitter and get away from the kids once in a while, and they were driving me right up the wall. It was on the day that my doctor told me I was pregnant with Child #3 that I hit my two-year-old so hard I blacked his eye. When he cried, I hit him again.

Clearly anyone who so emphatically does not want to give birth because she fears she will be abusive to any of her children should not be forced into parenthood. As for the unwanted child who may be targeted for abuse, I believe that it is far more immoral to condemn a child to a life that means certain torture and death than to simply terminate that life as early as possible.

Not surprisingly, Gloria Gillogley, who is head of a San Mateo-based Right-to-Life chapter, would disagree with me. When she was asked about abuse and the unwanted child by *San Francisco Examiner* reporter Jeanne Miller, she said, "We have only one issue—that killing a living entity is a violation of human rights. . . . Those who advocate abortion would rather say 'pro-choice.' It sounds less lethal, but for the helpless unborn child, there is no choice involved." Is there a choice for the baby tossed into a garbage can?

Or for the tiny, just-born baby for whom being tossed in a garbage can would have been a merciful alternative? I know you've probably seen pictures of aborted fetuses, but have you ever seen a battered baby? I have before me an eight-by-ten four-color photograph of a little tyke who couldn't be more than four weeks old. When I look carefully, as one must do when a child is spattered with blood, I can see that he's beautifully formed. The expression on his little face tells me that his last experience on this earth was one of total agony and terror—as I suspect all of his experiences must have been since his birth. His little body and face are covered with lacerations, bruises, and cigarette burns. His lovely curly brown hair is matted with congealed blood. I want to reach out and pick that baby up and gently wash him and wrap him in a clean blanket, breathe life back into his broken little body, and hold him, give him the love and comfort that is every child's birthright. Now, I may be abnormal, but I've never felt this way about an aborted fetus.

This beautiful child had a right, from the moment of his birth, to be loved and cherished. That right was violated by untreated mental illness and a lack of respect for him as a living human being, and society must bear part of the responsibility for his not having been protected against this horrifying violence. The fetus's right to life was maintained, but the child's wasn't.

Broken, living children make me weep. And the very idea that anyone would want to remove what few protections these young innocents have makes me rage. Under the guise of protecting the American family, the Religious New Right would not only condemn unwanted children to lives of horror and pain, but would remove any protection they now have, putting us back to where we were at the turn of the century, when there were no child abuse laws.

Mrs. Gillogley holds this view of child abuse: "We believe that abortion itself—the killing of unborn children—is the most extreme form of child abuse."

More extreme than continual battering? More extreme than bashing a baby's head in? More extreme than scalding a child for wetting his bed? More extreme than covering a child's body with cigarette burns? More extreme than roasting two babies on a grate to drive out the devil?

A question that used to plague me when I was involved with our hot-line program was why, with all of the talk of concern for aborted "innocent babies," never once in all of the years I was involved did a right-to-lifer ever step into our office and volunteer his or her services. But that was before I saw the gap that exists between the slogans and the practices, before I recognized the doublespeak that comes from people like Greg Dixon who say abortion is murder but children are born bad. The placard bearers who protest freedom of choice are cut from the same cloth as those who protest government involvement in child abuse cases. In Terre Haute, Indiana, the incident that had brought them out was the County Welfare Department's having removed from his father's care a nine-year-old boy who'd been severely beaten for lying.

Yes, I used to wonder why virtually every religion, with the exception of Fundamentalists and Mormons, was represented in the support of programs designed to prevent child abuse. But I don't wonder anymore. You must have a reverence for life—for living children—to be so motivated.

V

WOMAN AGAINST WOMAN, WOMAN AGAINST HERSELF

Women are not a class, they are a sex whose interests in a well-ordered government are represented automatically and inevitably by the men of their social group.

If the average woman is to be a voter, she must accept jury service and aid in the protection of life and property.

No question of superiority or equality is involved in the opposition to votes for women. The woman suffrage movement is an imitation of man movement, and as such merits the condemnation of every normal man and woman.

. . . To reinforce those who clamor for individual rights is to strike at the family as the self-governing unit upon which the state is built. . . .

Alice George
The Independent
October 11, 1915

It is often said that the chief obstacle to equal suffrage is the indifference and opposition of women, and that whenever the majority ask for the ballot they will get it. But it is a simple historical fact that every improvement thus far made in their condition has been secured, not by a general demand from the majority, but by the arguments, entreaties and "continual coming" of a persistent few. In each case the advocates of progress have had to contend not merely with the conservatism of men, but

with the indifference of women, and often with active opposition
from some of them. . . .

Alice Stone Blackwell
"The Indifference of Women"
February 1889

Our Severest Critics

Many reports tell us that no issue has so sharply divided American
women as the issues of equality and of reproductive freedom of
choice since women were pitted against each other over the right to
vote. Nearly three quarters of a century ago the arguments that
women used against women's suffrage were nearly identical to those
that are being used with respect to the central issues of concern to
women today. Alice George stated in 1915 the fear that women
would be dragged into military duty, that the movement was an "imitation of man" movement, and that suffrage would strike at the family itself—words nearly identical to those used by Phyllis Schlafly
more than half a century later. Were the current controversies over
our right to vote, those women who have fought against passage of
the ERA and continue to fight against freedom of choice and equality would no doubt be fighting against their own emancipation—their
own right to vote.

Some observers hold the view that the current division between
women has grown out of the battle between housewives and working
mothers. One of the conclusions drawn by Nancy Rubin in her
Ladies' Home Journal article was that career women have created
such deep feelings of resentment and inadequacy in housewives that
a backlash has them aligning themselves with anti-choice and anti-
equality organizations such as Stop ERA, the Pro-Family Action
Committee, the Eagle Forum, the National Right-to-Life Committee,
and the Moral Majority.

It is true that there exists animosity between working women and
housewives, and I believe there are many very human reasons for
this. One of them may be that all women have been so conditioned to conform, to look for our own validation in terms of what

others are doing, that when we see that someone else has chosen a different path, we don't get the affirmation of our identities we so need. And when someone has *rejected* that which we have chosen, we sometimes see that as some sort of personal attack. It is as simple as telling someone you don't like their car. But when the choice pertains to something more deeply personal and important to a woman—her whole way of life—the rejection is more keenly felt. Think for a moment about how some mothers feel when they learn that another woman does not want any children. Why in the world should that matter to them? It does, however, and unless it is part of their religion, those who judge other women for choosing not to have children do so because they feel that such a choice implies that motherhood is an undesirable state of being.

But when mothers are critical of other mothers, there's more to it. Some of the feelings of inadequacy some of us experience stem, perhaps, from the tendency in women to compare themselves to others—to use the accomplishments and competence of others as yardsticks for measuring their own worth. This habit of comparing ourselves to our peers seems to run deeper in women than it does in men. I recall that when I was newly married, for example, young women then vied for top honors in housekeeping by comparing themselves to others. This tendency, I believe, is rooted in the fact that traditionally there has existed one acceptable career for women—that of being a wife and mother. While men *do* compete, and no doubt compare, their range of options has been wider: Fred may be a successful lawyer, but Charlie is an engineer; Bill is the best stone mason in town, Harry is a very skilled carpenter. Furthermore, neither men themselves nor society in general have used as a yardstick for measuring a man's worth what sort of husband and father he is, beyond his being a good provider and a decent sort.

But since women have had until recently only one sphere of endeavor in which to excel, our entire sense of worth has been tied up in what sort of wives and mothers we are. As it is part of my own history, I know the litany well: Susan was smug because she breast-fed with more ease than I did—my limited success was validation of her superior motherliness; I was a better mother because my house was completely child-proofed, while Susan didn't care enough to put a gate in front of her cellar stairs; Sally was a better wife and mother because she kept a spotless house even though she had three small children; I was a better mother than Sally because I never locked my kids out of the house to keep it clean; Jenine was a better mother than Cecily, who put earplugs in her ears when the baby cried; I was superior because my "advanced" child cut a tooth at four months—until Steven, Maryann's baby, was potty-trained at five months. Really! On and on it went, and all of us, though some of us were more perfect than others, were better mothers than Laura, who returned to her job when her baby was six months old. Never mind that we didn't *want* to go back to work—the fact that we didn't have to (then) made us more caring mothers and less inadequate in our own eyes.

The housewife who perpetually thinks this way and then compares herself to working women may start to feel inadequate. "If *she* can spend full days working outside the home, that means *she* is more competent than I, as demonstrated by the fact that she is doing two jobs at once." Or she may think, "If *she* doesn't have to stay home that means what *I* do during the same period of time that she's away isn't necessary, useful, or important." This sort of self-indictment, or self-devaluation, keeps a woman from considering the possibility that the woman she's comparing herself to may not, in fact, *want* to work, and may be teetering on the brink of exhaustion because she must try to compress all those chores and obligations into the hours she's away from the office.

And then there's a component of *envy* when one compares. The housewife may, when she contrasts herself to the working woman spiffily dressed at 7:30 in the morning, conclude that her working peer has an exciting life because she's out in the world. She may then see her own life as dull and uninteresting by comparison and feel a trace of envy. "When I go downtown to run errands," a friend told me, "and I see all those gals on their lunch hours, nicely dressed, walking down the street with a sense of purpose, I feel a pang." We're not always apt to consider that their "sense of purpose" may be in achieving their goal of picking up a prescription, making a bank deposit, or buying socks for the kids—or any one of the dozens of errands that working women run on their lunch hours.

In contrast to the envy a housewife may feel, the working woman, with no flexibility in her schedule, may feel more than a trace of envy for the housewife who not only has some flexibility, but is her own boss. And certainly there is envy when she is scraping the windshield at 7:30 in the morning while her neighbor is inside the house still in her warm bathrobe. This envy became apparent to me when I told a neighbor I had returned to work and she said, "Good. Your days of being a lady of leisure are over. Now you're in the rat race just like all the rest of us." It became more apparent to me, however, when I was the woman scraping the windshield at 7:30 in the morning and another neighbor, still in her bathrobe, waved to me from her kitchen window.

Add to this low-level undercurrent of animosity mixed with envy the now frequently stated view that feminists in general, and working women in particular, *devalue* the housewife. One who said so publicly is Mary Tedrow, who told Nancy Rubin:

> I wonder, is it really inflation that drives so many women out of the house and back to work? A lot, I think, has to do with people wanting to live too high and wide. The problem is that our values are all screwed up. Women's lib really hurt the homemaker—it made us feel like we're nothing, like we're second-class citizens because we aren't working. . . .

Whenever I hear or read a statement like that, I am dismayed that the need to criticize mothers whose life-styles are different is so great that those who do so will second-guess the motives of the working woman. And I'm overcome with a compulsion to say, "Look, lady, you don't know anything about what it means to feel like a 'second-class citizen' until you have worked as a secretary to a male chauvinist pig, suffered a reprimand for being two minutes late to work, had to ask for permission to take a sick child to the doctor, suffered near-terminal boredom, and felt yourself to be locked into a terrible and demeaning job because you need the money."

The Source of the Blame

Furthermore, I would like to tell women who stand in judgment of all of us who work either out of need or choice that we are not the ones who are doing the devaluing of our more fortunate sisters at home. That particular shoe belongs on the foot of the man who, like my former employer, an ultraconservative male, holds the view that a woman's place is in the home while he deludes himself into believing that housewives do nothing but sit around and watch TV all day while their poor husbands slave to give them a good life.

For the record, the first time I became aware of this male view that housewives don't do anything was twenty years ago, when I heard an otherwise very nice man answer a question directed at his wife, the mother of their four young children. To, "Do you work, Sarah?" Sarah's husband saved her the trouble of responding and said, "No. She doesn't work. She's a housewife."

The male practice of putting down housewives is as old as the mother-in-law jokes that husbands seem to so enjoy. It is all part of an age-old practice of putting down women in general and is in the very air we breathe. It puts down the *people* who function in the housewife role, which puts down the role itself. The point is, it can be historically demonstrated that males have perpetually put forth the notion that motherhood is a piece of cake and housewifery a state that closely resembles retirement. This lack of recognition for all a wife and mother does, you may have noticed, manifests itself at the end of a mother's weary day of chasing preschoolers about and cleaning up dozens of messes in any one of the following greetings from her spouse: "What did you do all day?" "This house looks like it was shot out of a cannon." Or "What's wrong with you?" Such statements could only come out of the mouths of those who have no concept of all that is involved in the day-to-day supervision of children whose presence in the house makes housework all the more difficult and abundant. I do not wish to belabor a point we all know so well, but I must say again that only those who don't do it believe there's nothing to child care and housekeeping.

To those who hold the view that the women's movement is forcing women out of the house to overcome their feelings of inadequacy, I would like to mention the day my husband said, "Well, we just can't make ends meet. Looks like you'll have to get a job." The message couldn't have been clearer that being a homemaker was less important than being a money-maker. And who or what devalues the housewife when her homemaking activities are relegated to her off-hours and she herself is so devalued that no one seems to care that she has to rattle around until all hours of the night to get her chores done? Finally I would like to ask if it was "women's lib" that drove my friend Betty out of the house when her husband of twenty years left her for a younger woman, and she had to support herself and her son.

With all of the evidence to the contrary, where do women like Mary Tedrow get the idea that feminism is the villain? *Straight out of the mouths of people like Phyllis Schlafly and Jerry Falwell.* According to Jerry Falwell's preachings on *The Old Time Gospel Hour,* not only has feminism devalued the housewife, but it is the root cause of divorce because it pressures women to go to work to "fulfill themselves." He makes no mention of the fact that one of the major events that drive women out of the house is divorce.

The New Right leadership has managed to convince its flock that women are breaking up the family. Perhaps that's because there exists a view—fostered in large measure by the surviving feminine mystique—that when a woman leaves her husband, she's the wrong, but not wronged, party, and when it is the other way around, the same holds true. Ensuring that the blame remains on the same person regardless of the circumstances, people offer such disgusting clichés as "Well, if she'd made him happy, he never would have left her." Presumably she didn't clean the house, didn't prepare gourmet meals, didn't bow and scrape. Or if she did, then she let her appearance go. In truth she probably had the bad taste to grow older.

Thinking about this, I sat down one day and made a list of all of the lies about women that have been historically believed and promulgated. The role of the women's movement has simply been to expose these lies. Starting with the aforementioned lie, look at the catch-22 buried inside it: if a man leaves his wife, it is because she has let herself go. ("Boy, after the baby came, Mildred really let herself go. Who could blame Ralph for looking around?") But if she didn't let herself go (and, of course, didn't age noticeably), she could be seen as a temptress who invited sexual advances from other men—possibly rape.

Other lies that men and women have accepted in the past, and still do in good measure, despite the fact that we are supposed to have come a long way, are:

It's a woman's fault when she doesn't have a husband. "Can't get a man."

She's to blame when she cannot "give him a son," despite scientific evidence that males determine the gender of a child.

It's her fault when a couple can't have children.

She's abnormal when a couple agrees not to have children.

She's to blame when her children have problems.

It's her fault when she accidentally gets pregnant.

She's to blame when she's frigid, but he's to be pitied.

She's to blame when her husband is impotent, but he's to be pitied. "A real ball-breaker, that one."

When she works outside the home she's either materialistic, doing her own thing, or trying to avoid her responsibilities as a wife and mother.

When her husband wants her to work and she doesn't, she's lazy. Or incompetent.

It's her fault when her husband beats her. "She likes it." "She's a real bitch; she was just asking for it."

It's her fault when she gets raped. "She liked it." "She was asking for it."

On the other side of the ledger of the double standard, males are blameless. If a male is utterly rotten and there's no avoiding that truth, then it is because his mother or some other female made him that way.

As Florence Rush notes in *The Best Kept Secret* (1981), blaming women for what men do has evolved from "a long tradition of female archetypes such as Eve and Pandora who beset the world with evil." She goes on to point out very correctly the extent to which this is done when it comes to fixing the blame for male sexual abuse of their own children. Some modern therapists, sexologists, and criminologists, she tells us, assert that the tendency of some males to molest children sexually is caused by their mothers, that father-daughter incest is *instigated* "by the mother who is unwilling to sexually gratify her husband," and that some mothers do not adequately protect their own children. She cites the following appalling examples of how far some authorities will go to shift the blame of abuse from the guilty male to any woman lurking in the background:

One researcher described her incestuous father subjects as having broken a radio over a mother's head, burned the children with hot irons, locked a mother in the closet while sexually abusing their child, yet, nevertheless, concluded that a father's incestuous behavior is the result of "the failure of the mother to protect her child." This relentless tendency to blame women for male sexual transgression enabled Drs. Bell and Hall in their study *The Personality of a Child Molester* to attribute their subject's molesting behavior to his "fixation at an early age in psychosexual development due to his mother's intimacy." The doctors arrived at this conclusion even though Norman claimed that he might have gone on to college, a career and marriage had not his father sexually assaulted him when he was four.

Rush observes that because "mothers are seen as responsible for male violations, even child victims focus their rage against their mothers." That this psychological disease of mother-blame is so out of control is underscored for me by the fact that the researcher who blamed the mothers who'd been hit over the head with a radio or locked in a closet is a *woman,* Yvonne Tormes, attached to the Denver-based American Humane Association.

I think now of a man, no more than two years older than I, who has never stepped foot in a church or never looked at a Bible. He *forbids* his wife to work outside the home, blames her for all of his unhappiness, blames her because they have daughters and no sons, blames her because, horror of horrors, one of their daughters has become an electrician—he would rather she work as a secretary at $7 per hour than bring shame on him by doing "man's work" at $25 per hour. This man, who is about as religious as my pet cat, serves as a perfect example of how dogma-inspired patriarchy can touch us all. Naturally he has no great incentive to think things through because the system serves him very well. Not only are all of his needs taken care of by his obedient wife, but, inferior by many standards, he is superior to the "dummy" he married. He is a *man!* His wife, I must add, is no longer a *woman* because she has had a hysterectomy.

The masculine superiority mystique and its power base depend upon the systematic stripping away of a woman's self-esteem. And the culture can do it when and if there is no man around with finely honed skills. A woman who has been divorced for three years told me, "I've never been a real victim of sexism. I've had all of the advantages of a good education and parents who raised me to think well of myself and be independent. I have a career and plenty of money. But I haven't got a man. Even though intellectually I know better, I cannot shake off the deep conviction that without one I'm nothing."

"This is what patriarchy does to women," says Sonia Johnson. "Makes them helpless, makes them children and fools." Johnson points out that the basis for the patriarchy began millennia ago when it was set down in the Bible. But unlike other "good" Christian women, she stopped buying it. One day, she says, she made the rather "un-unique discovery that men had made God in their own image," and not the other way around, as the Bible asserts.

Fear and Envy of Women

While I believe that the ultraconservative fringe has an economic interest in keeping women down, it doesn't explain how and why it got started. We think males are superior to females because the Bible tells us so. But where did that information come from? From God? Jesus Christ? No, it came from those who *wrote* the Bible—men of their day. Was it God who inspired these men to write inequality into the Bible? I think not. At the core of this "divinely ordained" oppression of women lies an ancient and unhealthy jealousy and fear of women for the power we possess of reproducing the species.

Ashley Montagu provides lucid substantiation for this explanation. In his book *The Natural Superiority of Women* (1952), Montagu explains how the subjugation of women came to pass. Put simply, as the child bearers and the nurturers, females became more sedentary and confined to their caves, while the males, unencumbered by birthing and suckling, were not just responsible for going out and hunting, but also enjoyed considerably more freedom than females, which in ancient times (as is true today) gave them an edge of power. In other words men got the drop on women because of *situational* superiority.

But even having more freedom than females was not enough to mask the truth of female superiority, according to Montagu, so as natural as reproduction is, males had to turn it into evidence of weakness or inferiority. It came to be part of the folklore that childbearing was a handicap.

If one can turn childbirth into a handicapping function, then that makes women so much more inferior to the sex that suffers from no such handicap. Persons who resort to such devices are usually concerned not so much with the inferiorities of others as with their own superiority. If one happens to be lacking in certain capacities with which the opposite sex is naturally endowed, and those capacities happen to be highly, if unacknowledgedly, valued, then one can compensate for one's own deficiency by devaluating the capacities of others. By turning capacities into handicaps, not only can one make their possessors feel inferior, but anyone lacking such capacities can then feel superior for the very lack of them.

Ludicrous as the idea may appear to some, the fact is that men have been jealous of women's ability to give birth to children, and they have even envied their ability to menstruate.

And so we understand how menstruation came to be viewed as "the curse." It had to be put down because it was strictly feminine. However, Montagu describes tribes of aborigines who did not devalue menstruation but instead performed operations on their males so that they would imitate menstruation at certain rituals. And the way numerous Australian tribes have gotten around the issue of childbirth is to go so far as to assert that "pregnancy occurs in the male first, and that it is entirely dependent upon him whether the female becomes pregnant or not." In these tribes the husband dreams that a spirit child has entered him. "Should he desire a child, he tells his wife what has happened, and the spirit child is then transferred to her. Even then she is merely regarded as the incubator of the child planted in her by the male." I'd be willing to bet that the male waits until such time as the "incubator's" belly looks as if it can accommodate this "spirit child" before communicating to his wife that he wishes to do so.

But when childbirth cannot be falsely assigned to males, Montagu tells us,

> . . . [I]n almost all cultures pregnancy, birth, and nursing are interpreted by both sexes as handicapping experiences; as a consequence women have been made to feel that by virtue of their biological functions they have been biologically, naturally, placed in an inferior position to men. But as we today all know,

these biological functions of women are only minimally, if at all, handicapping.

It should, of course, be noted that having no control over how many times she will go through pregnancy and childbirth or how many children she will bear is the deciding factor in whether or not this natural function will be a handicapping one for the female. And that certainly puts another light on the biblical command to "be fruitful and multiply," doesn't it? The command itself implies that there may, in fact, be some choice in the matter, and that reminds me that we tend to forget that birth control is something that has been practiced since the dawn of civilization, not just since Syntex gave us the pill.

In any event, Montagu tells us,

It is worth paying some attention to the significance of the fact that in the fundamental role in which one would have thought it all too obviously clear that women were the superiors of men, namely, in their ability to bear and bring up children, women have been made to feel that their roles are handicapping ones.

If males generally, and perhaps unconsciously, have been jealous of the female's "natural superiority," it is more easily understood why *religious* males might be more inclined to build themselves up by downgrading women. Women have the same power as God in the creative sense that God created man—so does woman. Woman is more directly involved in the divine process of creation in a way that man can never be; who then really has a direct line to the creator?

In light of Ashley Montagu's ideas, it is interesting to look again at the twentieth-century view that holds *his* work to be more important than *hers*. As was discussed in Chapter One, in recent years that assumption has been made with respect to dual-career families. But long before that complaint surfaced, the feminine mystique gave rise to the idea that his work in an office or on a construction job was infinitely more important than hers, which involved responsibility for the life of another human being. Is there anything on earth *more* important than such a responsibility? Male supremacists argue quite well that their jobs support the family financially, and while that role is very important, it takes a woman to make the family. And in most instances, the actual *work* a woman does, to do that is more important than most jobs men do. But it has been easy to devalue her work because it doesn't generate any money.

But now, increasingly, women are doing their important mothering work *and* earning money doing something else. This very real threat to the myth of male superiority suggests the *psychological* reason for opposition to equality under the law. Women have very visibly offered proof that pregnancy and childbearing are not handicaps that render them inferior and that they can hold down jobs as well—no man can make that claim.

And now that women are starting to move a bit into the preserve of jobs that have always been designated as "men's work," the threat to male superiority becomes even greater. If, for example, a woman can be a trucker or an equipment repairperson or an electrical engineer—and a mother too—the suggestion that she is "inferior" falls completely apart, leaving the emperor standing there in his old invisible robes.

The complaint that women are taking men's jobs away from them takes on another meaning in this light, but it serves to mask what is really underlying the fears of those males who express it. And the women who buy into that complaint do so because the very basis of their belief system, hence their security, rests on the male superiority ethic. As Montagu says, the male envy of woman's physiological powers causes men to feel weak and inferior, and added to their jealousy is *fear*.

In the beginning this fear may not have been reasonable, but today it is. For if women ever collectively realize that they really do have power because of this unique capability, that they are still oppressed and that more and not less oppression threatens to be delivered, if they realize the reasons why it all got started in the first place, everything will change. Perhaps those men who most passionately want to maintain the patriarchal status quo sense that. Perhaps they also know that if a good Christian woman like Sonia Johnson can become aroused and join the ranks of the feminist movement, the awareness will spread like wildfire.

From this point of view alone it is not surprising then that the Religious New Right continually misrepresents to anyone who will listen the causes and effects of feminism. The new wave of feminism did not spawn the working woman. She has been around for a long time, and it was her accumulated disgust at being discriminated against in the work place that triggered the current wave of feminism. Just as capable as her male counterpart, she questioned why she was paid less and why she was passed over for promotions. No matter what the justification given, injustice makes normal human beings seethe. Add to the injustice in the work place the injustice in the home, and it is clear that the women's revolution of yesteryear and that of the sixties and seventies were both as inevitable as the American revolution and the civil rights movement. The first wave of the feminist movement—women's suffrage—and the more recent one came about because half of the population was (and is) being short-changed and lied to. The Religious New Right maintains that it is "natural" for women to be wives and mothers. It is also *natural* for the oppressed, when their rage, resentment, and indignation over injustices and lies have been bottled up for so long, to rise up.

The Myth of the Housewives' Backlash

"The idea was that women should unite in order to reach common goals," comments the *Ladies' Home Journal* in its introduction to Nancy Rubin's piece on the new "cold war" between women. "In practice, however," the *Journal* laments, "the events of the last decade may have done more to divide us than bring us together."

But the women's movement *did* begin to unify women. And while, on the surface, that promising beginning seems to have disappeared, as a mother and a mother-watcher I must say we have come a very long way from the time when the feminine mystique had us competing with each other so fiercely that there existed no possibility for any genuine closeness. Today's "cold war" is between housewives and working mothers, while yesterday's pitted housewife against housewife. Before feminism touched us, we were not open with one another, but in the last twelve or so years I have seen women of all stripes reaching out to share their universal concern with one another. I have seen the formation of support groups for parents, the forerunner of which I am now certain were the early consciousness-raising groups. Today we talk about how we feel while yesterday we simply played a game of Mine Is Better.

It is very clear to me that this promised unity is the last thing the

Religious New Right wants realized. Not only might the women in their own flocks start talking to one another, they might talk to "outsiders" as well. They might follow Sonia Johnson's example and start questioning their programming to such an extent that they will defect and join the ranks of their sisters and win the equality war. Quell the revolution before it gets off the ground! What the New Right has managed to do is expose an old wound inflicted by the patriarchy and pin a bum rap on the very people—feminists—who have been at the forefront in pointing out that the full-time housewife is one of the hardest-working and least appreciated women in America. What these manipulators of the truth have managed to do is rally the troops by (falsely) identifying the enemy.

The New Right—and the media—have created the impression, or the myth, that there exists a housewives' backlash. To understand that this isn't so, it is necessary to realize that offended housewives fall into two distinct camps: those who are somewhat defensive about their roles but are either supportive or neutral when it comes to the issues; and those who seem genuinely to believe all of the rhetoric of the New Right that holds feminism responsible for the decline of the American family and poses a very real threat to them personally. From all of my observations and research I find this latter group to be composed nearly exclusively of Phyllis Schlafly's supporters, members of the Mormon Church, members of Jerry Falwell's church, the John Birch Society, and other related organizations that make up the coalition of the New Right. In other words, there is no backlash; what we are seeing is simply the on-going battle of the far right, both old and new, one of the goals of which has always been the denial of personhood to women. Those people who are now fighting against equality and freedom of choice are essentially religious descendants of those who fought against granting women the right to vote. Naturally the New Right would like us to believe that all American housewives are in the battle. Clearly they are not. The very existence of the Homemakers Equal Rights Association, a large national movement, belies the simplistic conclusion drawn by a number of journalists that this is a battle between housewives and women who work outside of the home.

One of the founders of HERA is Ann Follis, the organization's first president. Some points she makes in her book, *I'm Not a Women's Libber, but . . .* (1982), underscore my view that rather

than devaluing the housewife, feminism has called attention to the
fact that our male-dominated culture historically has done so. While
we tout the glories of motherhood, culturally we put down those who
occupy the homemaking role. But more importantly, while homemakers have played an important role in the growth of our country,
their devaluation is carved in legal stone. Follis writes:

> The biggest shock of my life came when I began to discover
> the number of legal rights that women lose, depending on which
> state they live in, when they get married. It is perhaps the
> greatest betrayal of American womanhood that when a woman
> becomes a homemaker (which society encourages her to do) in
> doing so she may have actually *lost* legal rights and precious
> legal status that no other group in society is ever asked to relin-
> quish.

I must point out here that Ann Follis is a full-time homemaker,
the wife of a pastor, and a devout born-again Christian. But because
of her desire to help homemakers by fighting for equality, she has
been called a lesbian, a communist, and a man-hater by other so-
called Christian housewives, who have also accused her of "trying to
be like a man" and of not being a "real Christian" because her carefully studied interpretation of the Bible differs from theirs.

Ann Follis, it should be pointed out, is far from alone when it
comes to being a good Christian woman who is at odds with the
ultraconservative interpretation of woman's place according to the
Bible. The Evangelical Women's Caucus (EWC) is an organization
with chapters spread across the United States, and it supports equality for women. The organization's literature states that "The Scriptures ask both women and men to submit to *one another* [emphasis
mine]. . . ."

> We see much injustice toward women in our society. The
> church especially has encouraged men to prideful domination
> and women to irresponsible passivity. Our purpose, therefore, is
> to present God's teaching on female-male equality to the whole
> body of Christ's church and to call both women and men to mu-
> tual submission and active disciplineship.

The biggest hole in the conclusion that this "housewives' backlash" is the result of career women devaluing the homemaking role

centers around one issue alone: freedom of choice. I cannot imagine a housewife being motivated to join the so-called pro-life movement simply because the feminist movement has caused her to feel like a second-class citizen. *A majority of traditional housewives are pro-choice.*

The anti-choice activists are fanatical Christian women who are opposed to freedom of choice because their religious leaders have convinced them that abortion is murder and therefore a sin under any circumstances, and that not to work to change the existing legal status of abortion is tantamount to committing that particular sin. It has been my experience that activists who hold that view also hold not just the biblical view of woman's lesser status but the view that the Equal Rights Amendment calls for legalized abortion (among other things).

Equality of rights under the law shall not be denied or abridged by the United States or by any state on account of sex.

To believe that these words contain any advocacy of legalized abortion would require an inability to think.

The Brainwashed Flock

Sonia Johnson pulls no punches when she states flat out that the leaders in ultraconservative religious movements brainwash the flock and practice thought control.

Johnson describes her own experience when being under the spell of the Mormon Church as a condition of being only half awake, and her awakening as being like coming out of a deep sleep. Others who have been deeply tied to their churches express similar views as to their levels of consciousness. One former Fundamentalist, for example, said that she never was capable of having an original thought during the period when she was involved with her church. Another woman, an ex-Mormon, told me that, looking back, she could see that all of her life she'd existed in a fog. She said that after she left the church, she started to "stand up straight," explaining that she had been so "cowed" that she slouched for years and ultimately developed back trouble as a result. "The one thing people need to understand is that when you don't do what you're told to do, there are reprisals," she said. "A businessman in Utah, for example, may be threatened economically. Dealing with disobedient church women is easier—you simply disapprove of them, make them feel guilty, or threaten them with being alienated from the group."

It is not difficult to understand why such women would either passionately desire to believe what they are told to say, or, in view of the church's pervasive program to keep them utterly dependent, why they would be afraid to disobey, even if they feel otherwise. The women of the Mormon Church and other similarly structured ultraconservative churches, Johnson tells us, are more intensely programmed than most of us have been to believe that their very survival depends on their being married, and on being obedient to their husbands and the hierarchy of their churches. Indeed, in many instances it does, as church women are conditioned to be dependent and are not only discouraged from developing career skills that might make them financially independent, but are programmed to believe that they can never make it alone in the real world. Add to that the fact that these women are conditioned from birth to have many, many children, and it becomes even clearer how difficult it might be for them to be emotionally or pragmatically independent. Then there is the fact that their entire social life revolves around the church, which adds still another dimension of dependency.

When Sonia Johnson had her moment of truth—when she could no longer accept the idea that there was anything at all unchristian about the idea of equality under the law for women—and began questioning her church leaders about their position, she says they responded to all of her questions with either religious rhetoric, dismissal, or absurdities. Their general attitude, she says, was one that conveyed to her that neither she nor her questions were worth bothering about. When the hierarchy did indeed reply, its members insulted her intelligence by informing her that they were for equal rights, but not for the amendment. This sort of mutually exclusive statement she called "doublespeak." She was further insulted because she was required to accept it on blind, unquestioning faith.

When Sonia Johnson finally found out that the church hierarchy was holding meetings and planning strategies to block the ERA and then confronted them with the evidence, they denied it. They insisted that the *women* of the church were the ones who were "voluntarily" going to the barricades against the ERA, but they—the men—had nothing at all to do with it. In her book she offers abundant documentation for her claim that the strategies were set down entirely by the bishops and priests, that the church was pumping millions of dollars into their Stop ERA efforts, and that they were training women to debate the issue publicly, telling them what to say and how to say it. In other words, Johnson has said, what the women were recruited to do was "front for the men." Of those women who appeared to feel threatened by the ERA, she explained that they were only insofar as it was threatening to their men—the threatened men then had to force their women to oppose it to give the illusion that women actually opposed it. But even if they disagreed with their church's position, they would be afraid to disobey. There is much at stake in doing so, and they had before them the shining example of what had happened to Sonia Johnson when she did rebel and question. She was excommunicated from the church she loved, the church in which she had spent her entire life. That her husband left her for another woman may, in fact, have served as another example of what happens to women who step out of line—despite the fact that her husband's leaving reportedly had nothing to do with her involvement in the feminist movement.

Of her own dilemma and of women who have yet to face it squarely, Johnson writes:

> I am not significantly different from other women. If I had known the truth about women's condition all along, deep inside myself, then all women must know. But having accepted the patriarchal myth that they cannot survive in this world without male protection and approval, they struggle, as I did, to keep the knowledge of their oppression from their own consciousness. . . . I think I made my sisters' studied nonawareness more difficult to maintain, and threatened to wake them up and make them take responsibility, be fully adult and independent humans. I know many of them deeply doubt that they are capable of this; they are the ones my voice disturbed the most. They did not want to hear it. I don't blame them; neither did I for forty-two years. . . .

Probably the greatest hurt along the way for her was the realization that the bishops and priests she had trusted and believed for as long as she'd known them had lied to her, not only with respect to their position on the ERA, but also to the degree of their involvement in the church's movement in opposition to it.

Partly because of Sonia Johnson's experience, and partly because of the many untruthful statements of the Religious New Right in general, I no longer have any trouble accepting the idea that certain religious leaders lie when it suits their purposes. I wonder, however, whether devout Christian women would deliberately break the commandment that admonishes us that lying is a sin. It seems more believable that when they do not speak the truth they are either operating out of fear, blind faith, or programming.

Such pressures may have influenced a woman who challenged former senator Birch Bayh after he had given a speech at the Conference on Public Schools and the First Amendment in April of 1982. Bayh had followed the Reverend Tim LaHaye on the program, and while he had refuted some of LaHaye's allegations, he did so with respect and expressed no antagonism toward him. After he had finished speaking and had invited questions from the floor, a woman who identified herself as a "councilman" took the microphone and the following exchange took place:

". . . I really feel that we have a right to come to something like this and hope to hear an honest and factual discussion of divergent views without acrimony. I think your *slurs* toward Dr. LaHaye, who preceded you, really diminished your credibility."

"Did I slur him?" asked Bayh, who appeared to be genuinely puzzled. "I didn't mean to slur him."

"I felt you did," she snapped.

"I'm sorry," said Bayh. "I apologize to you and to him and to everybody else. I didn't mean to slur him. I just repeated what he said. Didn't I?"

"No, you didn't," she spat.

"Did I misinterpret what he said?"

As this exchange of "I didn't," "Yes you did" continued for about another minute, with Bayh looking totally bewildered, people in the audience were turning to one another and asking each other what they had missed. I heard no slur, I sensed no acrimony, nor did any of the people sitting near me. It was as if the woman who was accusing Bayh had not heard his speech. It occurred to me that in anticipation of an attack on LaHaye, she had been asked to get up and challenge Bayh, to discredit him, to point out to the audience his "rudeness." And then, when the anticipated attack did not occur, the woman's old program remained and she reacted according to it, without awareness that what she was saying was inappropriate. This idea turned into real suspicion when I later learned that the woman was a member of Phyllis Schlafly's Eagle Forum.

Later at that conference we heard from Janet Egan, co-founder of Parents of Minnesota, Inc., an organization that purportedly concerns itself with the quality of education in the public schools. In her prepared statement to the conference she explained that the public schools were falling down on their jobs because they didn't teach children morality and truth. Her truth:

> . . . Equality in relationship to God's creation is a non-entity! Equality is a man-made concept, not God-made. . . . There are no two equal men or two equal women in the whole of existence. . . . God created man and woman and designated their existence.

When Mrs. Egan focused her attention on the public schools more specifically, she told her audience about a third-grade reader published by Holt, Rinehart and Winston. She described a story entitled "How to Keep the Cousin You Hate from Spending the Whole Weekend at Your House and Maybe Longer," which she said teaches children how to outwit and manipulate their parents. She said that the instructions to the teachers noted that this teaches children psychological warfare.

Well, I called Holt, Rinehart and Winston and spoke with the editor who is in charge of elementary school books. She told me that yes, they had published the story about the cousin, but had nearly immediately deleted it from the text. The book had been published some five years earlier, and the story deleted nearly that long ago, so she couldn't understand why it was being mentioned at this late date. She also assured me that her company had never used the term "psychological warfare" as something that was taught to third-graders—or anyone else for that matter.

In session after session at that conference, my suspicions that there were programmed speakers and programmed shills in the audience grew. At one in particular the confusion began with the name of the speaker's affiliation alone. The speaker was Terry Dodds, who is

"Chairman" of the Eagle Forum's Committee to Stamp Out Textbook Censorship. Their definition of censorship: replacing thirty-year-old textbooks with updated versions. Their definition does not cover the "deleting" of material said to challenge "traditional family values."

The most memorable moment of this particular workshop came during a lull while Mrs. Dodds was unsuccessfully trying to arouse concern, or even belief, that secular humanism was being taught in the public schools as evidenced by some courses on values clarification and some schools' failure to teach children that a woman's place is in the home. To spice things up, a Mrs. Betty Young stood up and told a story about it being common practice in one public school to teach ten-year-old girls how to masturbate using a Coke bottle. Well, that certainly woke us all up!

I raised my hand, stood up, and asked Mrs. Young how she knew that to be a fact. She explained that she was not at liberty to reveal any more than she had already revealed. When I pressed further, it was suggested that if I took it up with Mrs. Young after the session, I'd receive the documentation I was asking for. I learned nothing more, however, beyond what she had already told the group: the name of the school district. The "reliable source," she explained, was the father of a girl who had the bad luck to be in this class, and he had confided in her. No, Mrs. Young couldn't give me the father's name, as my knowledge of it would somehow bring disgrace upon his family.

On my return to California I called the superintendent of the school district in what turned out to be a very traditional and small community (population 8,000), and he gave me his version of Mrs. Young's story. He explained that the incident that had caused a stir in his district took place some seven years earlier, and had occurred in a sex-education class when one of the students asked how girls masturbate. When the teacher attempted to answer the question, she realized that the subject was really out of bounds and instructed the class to direct such questions to their parents. This resulted in a meeting with parents and teachers to establish some ground rules for what would be appropriate for discussion in a group situation. He emphasized that no one had ever been taught how to masturbate using a Coke bottle. After he explained this to me, he said, "I know that Mrs. Young goes around the country telling this disgusting story. She couldn't have any direct knowledge of what goes on here, as she has never been in our district. I just don't know why she does it."

The Council on Mind Abuse (COMA) of Toronto has identified twenty-two mind-control techniques that are used by cults to maintain loyalty as well as adherence to the rules of a group. Of these I have identified fourteen as being commonly practiced by the Religious New Right. The subjects on which these techniques are practiced are most often women.

HYPNOSIS—A stage of high suggestibility initiated by hypnosis often thinly disguised as meditation: Conway and Siegelman (*Holy Terror,* 1982) supply one answer: "Fundamentalist mind control is not like bedrock cult methods that use nonsense mantras and empty chants to still the workings of the brain at neurophysiological levels," they write. But in the constant repetition of verses from the Scriptures, "the book becomes their secret policeman, an intimidating inner force of suggestion." Combined with literal adherence to the Scriptures, which impairs the individual's capacity to make reasoned, independent judgments, "the Bible may also act as a barrier to interaction with the larger world."

ISOLATION—Loss of reality induced by physical separation from the rest of society: In the Mormon and Fundamentalist churches isolation from the rest of society is fostered by having members' entire lives revolve around their church group. As Fundamentalist preacher Tim LaHaye advised his audience at a meeting on August 27, 1981, in Des Moines, one way to maintain a good Christian home and life is to avoid contact with people who are not members of the church. He said that Christians should make their number one priority after God giving up all outside activities and spending spare time at home with their families.

PEER GROUP PRESSURE—Suppression of doubt by encouraging the natural need to belong: The evidence abounds that this occurs in far right religious movements and churches. There is, according to Sonia Johnson, much more fear of group disapproval than in the outside world. One of the greatest fears is rejection for having different views or feelings, or for questioning the basic tenets of the religion or the edicts of the church's leaders.

REMOVAL OF PRIVACY—Loss of ability to evaluate logically by never allowing private contemplation: Journalist Kenneth C. Danforth calls Mormonism a "cell-soaking" religion. For example, he says, "the nights of the week are so taken up with church activities that the church publicizes—as an innovation—its official program of 'Family Home Evening' every Monday. The Saints, in other words, are so captive to the daily demands of their church that they formally have to set aside an evening in order to have time with the kids."

SLEEP DEPRIVATION AND FATIGUE—Disorientation and vulnerability created by withholding adequate rest or sleep: While not actually a church practice, I include this here because this is something to which traditional mothers are susceptible. It is called "the tired mother syndrome," and because my focus here is on women and because ultraconservative churches pressure women to be baby machines and total caretakers, I think it is proper to make note of it.

GAMES—Childlike dependency on the leader induced by conducting games with obscure rules: Picking "rules" out of the Scriptures to support absolutes while avoiding those passages that do not support them, and then insisting on strict literal adherence to the Bible has to constitute a game. It creates "childlike dependency on the leader" to set down which rules are to be followed. And certainly the patriarchy, which fosters dependency in women, makes the game all the more intense.

METACOMMUNICATION—Purveying messages within messages by emphasizing certain words or phrases in long, boring lectures: an excellent description of most Fundamentalist sermons.

CONFUSING DOCTRINE—Rejection of logic as a pledge of faith is fostered by lecturing on complex cyclical dogma, which no one could understand: Christianity, and the Bible, when presented as absolute truth, demand a suspension of logic. And, of course, as there are hundreds of contradictions in the Bible, the doctrine is confusing on that ground alone.

GUILT—Teaching of eternal salvation reinforced by discussing sins of the former life-style: Generally speaking, guilt is a tool widely used to keep the flock in general obedient, and to blame women in particular, as they are accountable for virtually every evil in existence.

FEAR—Loyalty to group maintained by threatening soul, life, or limb: The message is very clear that if you don't accept Jesus Christ as your savior and follow all of the absolutes laid down by the church, your soul will fry in hell for eternity; just as clear is that if you violate the teachings of the church or question their veracity, there is the very real possibility that you will get yourself excommunicated.

CHANTING AND SINGING—Non-cult input prevented by demanding repetition of songs, chants, or phrases when in the presence of non-cult ideas: Repeatedly it has been my experience whenever presenting my own view to the pious to receive as a "response" nothing but quotations from the Scriptures and religious rhetoric.

DISINHIBITION—Abdication of adult responsibility encouraged by advocating childlike behavior: what is commonly done to females by the patriarchy from the moment of birth.

FLAUNTING HIERARCHY—Acceptance of cult bureaucracy produced by promising advancement, power, and salvation: It would not be difficult to make a connection between a cult leader's promise that if a member does anything for the cause, however ridiculous or unnecessary, he or she will be rewarded, and the New Right's coercion of their women members to work to maintain their own oppression. And, of course, accepting whatever is stated as an absolute in exchange for salvation seems to be "flouting" the hierarchy of the rest of the world outside the cult.

FINGER POINTING—False sense of righteousness created by pointing to the shortcomings of the outside world: This happens every Sunday, and on virtually every day of the week. Fingers are pointed at feminists, secular humanists, liberals, moderates, communists, homosexuals, or anyone else who does not conform to the rules.

Listening Research, an organization composed of former cult members and psychologists, and one that both Philip Zimbardo and I are affiliated with, has put together a list of what constitutes a religion instead of a cult:

No deceit in recruitment
Allows freedom of thought and action
Promotes the family unit
Does not isolate its membership

Encourages general community participation
Interested in promoting development of the individual
Supportive, sympathetic, and understanding
Encourages thought before commitment for life
Welcomes criticism

The church of Jerry Falwell, the Latter-Day Saints, and all other absolutist churches I am aware of score on only two points: "no deceit in recruitment" and "promotes the family unit." While I'm not really certain of the former, I'm certain of the latter because, as stated earlier, there is no doubt in my mind that the New Right sees the family unit as a useful device.

The Puzzle of Phyllis Schlafly

Several years ago Phyllis Schlafly debated a representative of NOW on William F. Buckley's *Firing Line*. She told Buckley and the audience, "Even Dr. Emerson . . . conceded that ERA will do nothing for women in the field of employment, which is already done by the Equal Employment Act of 1972." However, when Lisa Cronin Wohl contacted Dr. Emerson, a professor at Yale Law School, he told her, "No, I didn't say that at all. That's absolutely incorrect. Obviously ERA would do a great deal to improve opportunities for women workers." Writing in *Ms.* magazine (March 1974), Wohl observes, "But the television audience didn't have a chance to hear Thomas I. Emerson's corrections. Schlafly emerged unscathed and smiling and one step ahead of the facts."

Wohl gives another example that reinforces her point. It seems that when Phyllis Schlafly went to testify in Tennessee against the ERA, she kept waving around an article authored by Yale attorney Gale Falk. She repeated points that weren't in the article at all. Falk, who happened to be in the audience, finally rose from her seat in protest and corrected Schlafly's misrepresentations. But about a month after the incident Falk went to hear her testify in West Virginia and later told Wohl, "Exactly the same thing happened. She must not have noticed me—I wore a different dress and my hairstyle was different—because she repeated the same inaccuracies." There is no way of knowing how many times such misrepresentations occur without having someone present who can and will correct them, and so the myths are promulgated and believed by the faithful.

If one doubts that the women who work to maintain their oppression are mind-controlled, one needs only to look at Phyllis Schlafly and those who unquestioningly follow her. Anyone with her wits about her would straightaway question Schlafly's position that a woman's place is in the home when she herself has never been a housewife but has had a genuinely glittering career.

During the fifties she was a researcher for red-baiting Senator Joseph McCarthy, and she worked with the Cardinal Mindszenty Foundation, which is a right-wing Catholic anticommunist group. In the sixties she was active in Young Americans for Freedom, the John Birch Society, the American Committee to Free Cuba, Eagles are Flying and its Eagle Trust Fund (right-wing women's groups), Americans for Law and Order, and managed to squeeze in, during this period, writing two books and establishing "The Phyllis Schlafly Report." Always active in the Republican party, she once ran for Congress (when her youngest child was two years old) and also ran for the presidency of the Federation of Republican Women. During the seventies she formed the National Committee to Stop ERA and made working for it a full-time job that involved a great deal of travel. This mother of six children was involved with Stop Immorality on TV and a number of other right-wing organizations and still managed to write another seven books, not to mention becoming an attorney along the way.

As a mother of just two children who has been active in community affairs and also writes, I bow down to Mrs. Schlafly in utter awe. There is absolutely no way I could keep up with one tenth of such activity. She is truly superwoman, worthy of being profiled in *Ms.* magazine as a woman of incredible accomplishment and energy—to say nothing of being a role model. In fact, when she ran for the presidency of the Federation of Republican Women, she and her supporters carried signs reading MEN IN THE PARTY WANT WOMEN TO DO MENIAL WORK AND NOT MAKE POLICY, which gives her surprising credentials as a true feminist.

She has always advised her own daughters to develop career skills in case they have to work, and she says that if a mother has actual financial need, she should get a job instead of becoming a welfare recipient, something she likens to being nearly a card-carrying communist. In the same breath she says that a woman's place is in the home. The women who follow her don't seem to notice the contradiction.

Generally what she says and what she does, in fact, confuse those who attempt to find a thread of consistency; and those who don't look for that thread but march into battle in a stupor are in awe of this woman who they believe is fighting for their rights as homemakers. As Juanita Barnett told Alan Crawford, they are so devoted that they would "kill" for Phyllis Schlafly. And how does Mrs. Schlafly reward such devotion? In the name of God, the country, the flag, and motherhood she tells her pathetic and devoted followers that an equal rights amendment won't do anything for women. She should instead have been telling them all along that such an amendment would make it unconstitutional for women to be discriminated against in about 1,600 different ways.

She should have been pointing out to these women in the farm states who trust her that if they die first, their husbands pay no inheritance tax on the farm, but if the husbands die first, the wives *do,* as a man's farm is considered "his" farm. It might be similarly helpful for such women to be told that if they don't live in Arizona, California, Idaho, Louisiana, Nevada, New Mexico, Texas, or Washington, they do not have the benefit of community property laws.

This leader of homemakers should have been telling women that should they ever live in Arkansas and have to work to put food on the table, there's a law that prohibits women from working in mines; if they live in Mississippi, there is a maximum number of hours women may work, thereby reducing the amount of overtime already underpaid women can earn. They are similarly discriminated against in New Hampshire, and Ohio prohibits women from being gas or electric meter readers, bellhops, pinsetters, or cab drivers.

If they are not too brainwashed to hear it, certainly these women might be interested in a law in Alabama that states that a man who kills his wife in the act of adultery is guilty of manslaughter, while when the situation is reversed, the wife is guilty of murder. Awakened, she could have incited women to riot over a law in South Carolina that holds that if a wife flees her home because of physical abuse and then files for divorce, she must prove her life was endangered and that she did not "provoke" the abuse.

One on top of another, hundreds of laws maintain women as second-class citizens. One in Maine holds that if a couple jointly runs a business, no matter how hard the wife works, all of the profits belong to the husband. I cannot possibly list all the laws that discriminate against women economically, and that leave dependent wives in the lurch when their husbands choose to trade them in on new models. These are the things that any defender of American women should have been telling her audiences.

But Schlafly told them the ERA would do nothing for them. She failed to mention that when the state of Pennsylvania put an ERA into its own Constitution, three hundred laws had to be changed because they discriminated against either men or women.

Instead she told the faithful that their daughters would be forced into combat. Because this issue seemed to go straight to the hearts of the women who believed her and because her assertion was untrue in so many ways, I must digress. The fact of the matter is that although some mild protection against women being conscripted exists as a result of the Supreme Court approval of an all-male draft, please note that *without* the existence of an Equal Rights Amendment, the Court *did not outlaw a coed draft*. Not only did Mrs. Schlafly fail to mention that small detail, she also failed to mention that, despite the fact that women do not have equality under the law, the United States Congress is empowered to, at any time there is a national emergency, call for the induction of both able-bodied men *and women*. A final irony in Schlafly's using the draft as a device and it being believed is that now, according to Ellen Goodman, many months after the defeat of the ERA, the Department of Defense has got together a proposal to draft women. They want to draft women doctors, nurses, pharmacists, physical therapists, and other health-care professionals. If you are tempted to say, "Yes, but these personnel are never sent into combat," then you have never seen *M*A*S*H*. As Goodman wrote in her March 11, 1983, *Boston Globe* piece, ". . . folks at DOD made a special distinction. Nurses, they said, were not in combat roles. They should tell this to the Army and Navy nurses of other wars, especially 100 nurses who were prisoners of war for three years during World War II, or the female veterans of Vietnam." As an aside, even though my personal opinion is that no one should be drafted and that war is totally immoral, if men are going to be trained to defend themselves in the event of war, then women should be trained as well. Why should women be left at home, helpless and defenseless, when the plunderers come, as the New Right predicts they surely will?

Schlafly struck fear in these already fear-ridden, esteem-robbed victims of patriarchy by telling them that passage of an ERA would automatically mean that we would have unisex public restrooms. And they never questioned it, never stopped to think about the fact that in order for that to occur, there would have to be a consensus of people who wanted it and that a court ruling would probably be necessary. No one ever asked, "Who is going to go to all that trouble over bathrooms?"

She managed to convince her followers that they would be dragged from their homes and forced to work, an idea that any thinking person knows is utterly absurd. She told them that career women take jobs away from breadwinning husbands, but neglected to mention that many mothers work because the "breadwinner" ran off and left no forwarding address, and that this might someday happen to them. Even though most women work as secretaries and clerks and few men apply for those positions, she managed to get her message across to them: "These libbers are out to take your husbands' jobs away from them."

Of all of Schlafly's most outrageous public statements, I nominate for top honors the proclamation that for "the virtuous woman," sexual harassment is not a problem "except in the rarest of cases. . . . Virtuous women are seldom accosted by unwelcome sexual propositions or familiarities. . . ." She managed to indict most rape victims while she revealed that she knows absolutely nothing about the modern work place. From what I've seen, sexual harassment is rampant, and unfortunately most who are targets of it do not have the time and the energy to take the matter to the personnel department or a court of law. Shame also makes many victims reluctant to take legal action.

Finally, after the ERA was defeated, she repeated her old line and developed a new one when she said, "The ERA didn't pass because the American people did not want American women drafted. . . . The American people do not want irrational sameness of treatment between men and women. We want to be able to treat men and women differently in those areas that are different." A simple amendment that called for equality—nothing more—and she blows it all out of proportion while ignoring the fact that the majority of Americans did want it, the Congress approved it, and thirty-five states—a majority, for those who can't add—ratified it.

The secret of Schlafly's dubious success, according to Juanita Barnett, a Republican activist from Illinois, is the conservative men who have given her "a platform and let her be the spokesman on the issue." As she told Alan Crawford, "Phyllis can say things no man could ever get away with. She serves their cause and they use her in full knowledge of what they are doing. She is the biggest tool that conservative men who want their women barefoot and pregnant have." In the process of leading the Stepford Wives into battle, she herself serves as living proof of that tired old male allegation that women are irrational.

The biggest question about Phyllis Schlafly is *why*. What's in it for her? The most obvious answer, of course, is that the male cause has served her well by turning her into one of the most famous women in America. But I think there's more to it. Do her outrageous positions and preposterous statements suggest that, in the final analysis, Schlafly herself, like an articulate Moonie recruiter, is putting forth the ideas of a true believer?

VI

SEX, DRUGS, ROCK AND ROLL—NOW IT'S TIME FOR MIND CONTROL

. . . our children in the government schools have been subject to possibly the most subtle yet intense brainwashing that any generation of children in the free world have ever experienced.

. . . Through sex education our children have been sensitized, through values clarification they have been moralized, through death education they have been animalized, now through environmental education they have been zombie-ized. No wonder, with few exceptions, they walk like cattle into rock concerts to be paganized, and sit before their televisions and become robotized. Why would *anyone* think they would not be ready, through global education, to be communized, Red Chinese style.

Greg Dixon
Conference on the First Amendment and
the Public Schools, April 21, 1982

TITLE IV—VOLUNTARY PRAYER AND RELIGIOUS MEDITATION
FINDINGS

Sec. 402.(a)   The Congress finds that—

(1) America is a Nation founded on freedom;

(2) essential to freedom is the free exercise of the inalienable rights guaranteed to all by our Creator;

(3) in order to preserve such rights it is equally essential that the Constitution be broadly interpreted in matters of individual freedoms; and

(4) the free exercise of religious expression whether public or private is a fundamental freedom which should not be benignly denied in order to protect other freedoms equally fundamental.

The Family Protection Act, S. 1378
authored by Senator Roger A. Jepsen

Exploiting the Fears of Parents

If you were to ask the first ten people you meet on the street whether they approve of that section of the Family Protection Act that calls for a return of voluntary prayer to the classroom, probably two or three would say that they do not and would base their objection on the fact that America is the home of people of many different religions. They would no doubt tell you that Christian prayer would discriminate against non-Christians and that it would be impossible to find a prayer that would be suitable for all children and that no child should be forced to draw attention to himself or herself by asking to be excused while a prayer was being said. Or they might tell you that since the Supreme Court ruled on the matter back in 1962, to pass legislation that would allow school prayer would dilute the authority of the Court or put the Court in conflict with the Constitution.

However, if recent polls are any indication of public sentiment, seven out of ten of the people who had the question put to them would probably approve of having prayer back in the public schools. Most American adults don't worry a great deal about Constitutional matters, and those who consider themselves to be Christians aren't always apt to imagine how those who aren't might feel about the issue. Certain Americans concerned about the morality of our young people would like to see the injection of a little Christianity into the classroom and feel that a little prayer or religion might help keep children on the straight and narrow.

I felt that way myself a few years back when my children hit adolescence. "Maybe," I said to a friend, "what we need is some old-time religion." I spoke as a frightened parent who was about to come up against sex, drugs, and rock and roll. It was here—the dreaded teen period I'd heard and read so much about. Having little faith that my husband and I had the ability to meet this trying time head-on, I would have welcomed some magic institutionalized formula to get us through it.

The problems had been fully identified for me long before the Religious New Right came along to spell them all out, although I sometimes have the feeling that some of the leadership think they were the ones to discover them. Although they are on target in stating some of the *dimensions* of the problem, they are simplistic when it comes to the underlying causes: permissiveness has spawned feminism, which has led to the breakdown of the family, opening the door for pornography, the erosion of our educational system, and the proliferation of rock and roll music, all of which has led to teenage promiscuity, drug abuse, alcoholism, depravity, perversion, and crime in the streets, etc. The problems and the causes thus identified, the New Right had a tidy piece of legislation in the Family Protection Act, which, as you've seen, covers a lot more than school prayer, and promises to clean up America once and for all.

And people are buying it, mostly sight unseen. Even the most *untraditional* parents, according to pollster Daniel Yankelovich, whose agency measures the public pulse, find some appeal in the New Right's formula for morality—when it comes to their children. Writing in *Psychology Today* (November 1981), he says that "those who stress self-fulfillment and deemphasize money, work, marriage, and obligations to others nevertheless raise their children according to traditional moral precepts, and are about as likely to teach their children that duty comes first and sex outside of marriage is morally wrong."

That there exists quite a lot of sex outside marriage to alarm such parents is a statistical fact. According to the Alan Guttmacher Institute 1.4 million teenagers become pregnant each year. The nightly news tells us that drug abuse and crime are rampant and brings rape and murder into our living rooms, along with advertisements for burglar alarms. Parents do not have to read the volumes of studies that are cranked out to know that one of the reasons our children are in deep trouble is that the quality of public education continues to erode, seemingly with every passing day. Parents start to worry when they notice that their fourteen-year-olds don't know the difference between *to, two,* and *too.*

What Falwell and Company are doing is taking advantage of the opportunity that our more visible social problems have collectively presented. Using them to arouse fear in parents by magnifying them out of all proportion, they have obscured from view not only what their genuine motives may be, but what really might underlie these problems.

Sex Education Has a Long Way to Go

The great panaceas in the Family Protection Act that will allegedly stem the tide of "promiscuity" are those provisions that would deny access to birth control to minors without parental consent and prohibit sex education in the public schools. According to New Right wisdom these are two of the primary things that are encouraging or fostering teenage sexual activity.

I have seen an expression of sudden recognition light up the face of more than one mother when it was pointed out that teenage pregnancy and out-of-wedlock births have risen since sex education was introduced into the public school system. As one woman, after reading that Phyllis Schlafly had stated flatly that this *proves* that sex education *causes* pregnancy, told me, "She may be a nut, but she does have a point."

Does she? Not according to psychologist Sol Gordon, she doesn't. Dr. Gordon says in *Impact '82–'83,* published by the Institute for Family Research and Education, "I would like to remind those who are not familiar with statistics that two phenomena coexisting do not prove causality. For example, the time in the United States when school prayer was most widespread was also the time of the Great Depression. That does not prove that school prayer caused the Depression." What the coexistence of these two phenomena suggests to me is that first, although sex education exists in *some* schools, not all teenagers take such courses (they require parental consent) and next, that the courses being taught don't adequately explain reproduction.

According to the Alan Guttmacher Institute, for example, forty-one percent of all teenagers who got pregnant thought they couldn't conceive because it was the wrong time of the month, they were too young, or it couldn't happen the first time.

An example of how badly we all might educate our children can be seen in my own daughter's perception of menstruation when she was twelve years old. When she asked me if getting her period would mean that she would have a baby, I repeated my well-rehearsed (and rather good, I thought) routine on the miracle of reproduction. I was dismayed at her growing impatience until finally she exploded: "You aren't answering my question!" What was the question? "Does this mean I'm going to have a baby?" What she was asking, I suddenly realized, was if getting her period would cause her to have a baby. When I said, "No," she walked away in utter relief. But later on her relief seemed to be replaced with depression. When I asked her why she was so upset about having her period, she told me that she didn't think she could stand to bleed every day for the rest of her life.

Another example of how sex education goes awry can be seen in what the twelve-year-old son of a friend of mine told his mother about what he had learned in class as to how conception occurs. When she pressed him for an explanation, he said, "With the man's penis, or with a finger—but only if the finger is in the Virginia."

Although the figures on teenage pregnancy are staggering, careful consideration of the matter suggests that we cannot be certain whether these statistics reflect an actual increase in either the *rate* of sexual activity or the *rate* of pregnancies that occur prior to marriage. For one thing, the statistics themselves are something new. As recently as fifteen years ago there existed no accurate reporting of teenage pregnancy: we now have statistics on abortion, for example, something we didn't have before the Supreme Court struck down the prohibitive laws, as no records were kept on illegal procedures unless they were botched and resulted in death or hospitalization. There was no Alan Guttmacher Institute around to keep records on how many teenagers practiced birth control. And we have no way of knowing how many teenage pregnancies were hidden from the data-collecting process during the days when "nice" pregnant girls nearly always got married. Finally, those pregnant girls who didn't get married but instead gave their babies up for adoption were usually admitted to hospitals as married women, and the births reported as legitimate.

Taking this a step further, I sat down one day and made a list of twenty women I had known during the fifties when we were in high school together. I selected for my sample girls who came from the very best and most traditional middle-class families, whose parents had remained married to each other, and whose families were affiliated with some established religion. While we did not have the pill, and it was nearly impossible for girls to obtain diaphragms, birth control was practiced in those "dark ages," as boys still carried condoms in their wallets.

Out of this group of twenty "nice" girls, four were sexually active before marriage, evidenced by the fact that they got married because they were pregnant, some while they were still in high school.

Of the remaining sixteen girls, I happen to know for a fact that half of them were sexually active before marriage because they shared their guilty secrets with me. *All others* married before their nineteenth birthdays, with the youngest unpregnant one marrying at age fifteen. It is my guess that those who married young but were not pregnant exemplify the phenomenon Betty Friedan reported—that the feminine mystique enticed women into marrying and having children at increasingly younger ages. It may also reflect the fact that many women of my generation married simply because of the external and internal pressures to have sex. As one woman told me, "I was a virgin when I got married for the first time, and I got married only because I wanted to go to bed with my boyfriend."

People don't marry for that reason any longer—at least not as much as they once did—but people *do* talk a lot more about sex than they did when I was growing up. It is no longer shameful for someone to admit to sleeping with someone she loves. It should be pointed out, however, that even those who may admit to doing so will frown on what my daughter calls "slutting around." Most of the young people I know hold the view that sex without love is something people do for "cheap thrills."

In an effort to measure what might be typical attitudes and mores in the United States today, Peter Davis sought out the American town that might best represent current American traditions—one with sufficient ties to the past, yet progressive enough—and settled on Hamilton, Ohio. He studied Hamilton and its people for four years, the result of which is his fascinating analysis *Hometown* (1982). Some observations he makes are that the change in sexual attitudes from Puritan days has been complete in that we can now talk about sex and read about sex, "as long as one remembers that sex was and remains an American obsession." Yet "there is still a great deal more talk than action in Hamilton. The double standard itself rides on, boys 'gaining' sexual experience while girls 'lose' their virginity."

We simply know more today about sexual activity. Sar A. Levitan, coauthor of the book *What's Happening to the American Family,* told Robert F. Buchanan (*Los Angeles Times,* October 16, 1981):

> What I'm saying is that so often it's the public perceptions that change and not what is actually happening. Premarital conception, for example, is not new. An estimated one third of the recorded births in Concord, Massachusetts, during the two decades prior to the Revolution were conceived out of wedlock. This is roughly the same proportion as in recent years.

"Yes, but," you may be saying, "they're starting so much younger now." How in the world do we know that to be a fact when traditionalists are reluctant to state that they were sexually active before they got married? Besides, if they are starting younger, there's a good reason for it. The age of puberty has gotten progressively lower during the past one and one half centuries. The latest survey, conducted at Harvard University, reviewed 218 reports on puberty in the United States and Europe. In general it was found that the age of puberty has declined by two or three months each decade.

A fresh approach to the problem was offered by Caryl Rivers in the *Los Angeles Times,* December 15, 1981:

> . . . The girl who receives early training in independence and assertiveness has a chance of not falling into the trap of premature motherhood. •
> . . . If you examine the sexual behavior of teenagers, you find that, for girls, the driving force is not libido but the need for love and acceptance.
> . . . It is very hard for a teen, at an age when peer pressure and the desire for male attention is intense, to insist that she will set her own timetable for when she will engage in sex. And if she decides that she is ready for sex, she probably has to take

the initiative in insisting on contraception. To do this requires a sense that she can and must control her own destiny. The ability to make demands, handle conflicts, plan ahead—these are not qualities that a girl can develop overnight at puberty. Yet too often we do not train our girls early in these traits.

I would venture to suggest that the least assertive of all are those who are in homes where they are taught that they must obey their parents in all things, and thus become generally obedient toward anyone who they perceive as being superior or a higher authority. What a bind that is for a young girl who is programmed to believe that males, by virtue of their gender, are authorities and that they should be submissive to them or defer to them.

Girls who are caught up in this bind, according to Caryl Rivers, who studied the matter with psychologists Grace Baruch and Rosalind Barnett of Wellesley, transfer their dependency from their parents to their boyfriends. "They get pregnant 'by accident,' not really understanding that they have any responsibility for or control over what happens in their lives."

"All of the sex education in the world," concludes Rivers, who has collaborated with Baruch and Barnett on the book *Beyond Sugar and Spice* (1981), "will not put a real dent in the pregnancy rate if we can't persuade young girls that they can—and must—control their future, not merely collide with it."

From these observations we can see that the New Right has missed the mark by a mile—the chastity they exalt may in part be dependent on the feminism they so condemn. In twisting the facts to support their rhetoric the New Right winds up obscuring from view possible solutions to the very problems over which they express great concern.

Before dealing with misrepresentations as to the causes of some of our other social problems, I would like to dwell for a moment on the question of promiscuity. I define promiscuity as being perpetual and indiscriminate sexual activity, not an act that takes place between young people who are in love with each other. While it may be a good idea for teenagers not to engage in sex because often they lack the maturity required to handle mature relationships, I simply cannot find it in my heart to brand a seventeen-year-old girl as being "promiscuous" when she has sex with her boyfriend. I realize that this would shock the designer socks off of Jerry Falwell, but I must say that I would rather my own daughter do that than repeat the mistake of the mystique generation—marrying too young simply to avoid sinning, and then either divorcing or living out lives of quiet desperation because it was a marriage that shouldn't have taken place at all.

While there is too much emphasis on sex generally, the openness that exists today is far healthier than the narrow-mindedness that had women of my generation believing that sex was sinful—a notion that many of us brought to our relationships with our husbands whether or not we slept with them before marriage. Our attitudes were so screwed up, it would require an entire book to detail them and, in fact, has inspired a number of them.

A final observation: Whenever the New Right yammers about sexual morality, females are the focus of attention. Males are never promiscuous? It's all right for males to be promiscuous? Sexually active females have to have partners, you know. But only females are "sinners." They are the ones who, it is proposed, must have parental consent to obtain contraceptives. And should they be denied access to them and access to safe abortion, they are punished with pregnancy and weighty decisions about what to do with the baby, while those who would get them pregnant get off scot free.

Beyond Drugs and Sex

Another villain that the New Right has identified is, of course, rock and roll music. As Falwell says in *Listen America!,* "Not only are the graphics of album jackets often pornographic, but lyrical images are often conveyed in a code language known by teens who listen to rock music." He then quotes his authority, Bob Larson, author of *Rock,* to warn parents that "Some top hits are so lewd that the lyrics can't be printed [in his book] for fear of having this book classified as pornography." But they can be sold over the counter? Broadcast over our airwaves?

As the kids would say, gimme a break.

"Not only does rock music promote promiscuous sex," says Falwell, "but it has done much to advance the drug culture."

In focusing on drugs and rock music, Falwell et al. deliberately overlook one possible reason why some teenagers may not only be sexually active earlier than we think they ought to be, but also why they may do a lot of other things we'd rather they wouldn't do. I wish I could share the following conversation I had with my daughter not only with Mr. Falwell, but with the President of the United States.

It was a beautiful sunny California day. As my daughter approached me to talk, I thought about how she had metamorphosed. She had got through her awkward stage, shed her baby fat, her thick glasses, the braces on her teeth. I smiled at her loveliness until I noticed that it was marred by a shadowy expression on what I thought ought to be a carefree young face. When I asked, "What's wrong?" a tear slid down her cheek. I held her for a moment, stroked her hair, and urged her to talk.

"I don't have a boyfriend, Mom. Everyone has a boyfriend but me."

"Don't worry, honey," I told her, relieved that the problem wasn't critical. "Your time will come."

"Did you ever feel like this, Mom? Just like crying, and sad and stuff?"

"When I was your age?" I laughed. "Many times."

"Did you ever get scared at night and think you wouldn't wake up in the morning? I'm scared I'm going to die."

"It's not the boyfriend thing, then," I said.

"Mom, did you ever worry about dying when you were my age?"

"Yes. It's normal to think about such things."

"But, Mom, it was different for you."

"How so?"

"Mom, it's the war thing. There's going to be a war. Nobody can live. It's going to be terrible. They didn't have that when you were my age."

"Yes, they did," I said. But, I thought, I don't remember it being so bad. I remembered Korea, but I also remembered that there was a certain amount of restraint. The memory fades, but I don't recall our president talking about dropping nuclear bombs while doctors tried in vain to make him understand that treating survivors of a nuclear war would be impossible.

"It's not the same, Mom," my daughter said.

"No," I had to admit, "it's not."

"You see, Mom, I want to have a boyfriend before I die."

Then I understood. Apart from the fact that females now claim the right to behave as males have always behaved, I can see clearly why some of our young people see no point in waiting to try their sexual wings. While she is sensitive, my daughter is one of the most stable people I know. And her values are clear-cut—she absolutely does not believe that love and sex are separable, and she would not allow herself to be used or pressured. But too often for my comfort she does not see that she has a future. She has told me that she would like to live long enough to become a mother and then turned around an hour later and told me that she wouldn't bring a child into such a terrible world. And this is a pervasive attitude among too many young people who come through this house. They seem to be echoing Paul Ehrlich's remark that "If you've booked passage on the Titanic, you may as well go first class."

Ehrlich was referring to the mess our environment is in when he made the remark, and now that a cloud of nuclear war hangs heavy over the heads of our young people, it is doubly pertinent. In a discussion with a number of my children's friends, there was a general consensus that "If the bomb doesn't get you, pollution will." As one boy remarked, "What difference does it make if I cut school or go to class? What difference does it make if I get good grades? What difference does it make if I spend a week stoned out of my mind? I'm not going to live very much longer." He was not referring to having been told that he had a terminal disease. But for the way some of these kids feel, you'd think they'd just been put on notice by the medical center. Indeed, in a way they have. As Dr. Helen Caldicott wrote in her essay, "This Beautiful Planet,"

> The Harvard psychiatrists' recent study of 1,000 adolescents in Boston shows that one of the main reasons they think the children are taking drugs and drinking alcohol is that most of these children expressed a profound fear of the future and a feeling that they probably won't grow up and will never survive to have children.

When I think the unthinkable, it makes me temporarily berserk; and then I am filled with immense grief at the thought that the utter annihilation of life is all too possible. But I have lived. I have married, known love, had children, written books, worked in causes, had rich friendships, walked miles and miles along sandy beaches. I have no idea how I could tolerate such an idea were I just sixteen or eighteen or twenty.

I had a chance conversation not long ago with a thirty-one-year-old woman who told me, "I grew up with the bomb. We did drills and all of that. I guess the reason why my thirtieth birthday never bothered me is that I'm just surprised I'm still here. I never expected to see twenty." She was a sixties kid, a member of the protest generation, and she had protested. She also told me that after she left her family home at seventeen to go to college, the first thing she did was pick up a guy at the bus depot for her first sexual encounter. In college, she studied—"Just in case we might survive after all"—smoked dope, dropped acid, and sniffed cocaine. "I saw no reason not to," she told me. "And it made the unbearable more bearable."

Legacy of the Mystique

Even if we can manage to assure our children that they might have a future and that it is therefore a bad idea to fry their brains on drugs or rush into sexual relationships, just reinforcing that and dealing with them on a day-to-day basis has become overwhelming. Even parents of teenagers who stay out of trouble seem to have difficulty simply coping with teenagers. While this has probably been so since the dawn of civilization, I think it is worse now because parents—especially mothers—have been under more pressure than ever before. Along with the baby boom and the feminine mystique came the child-centered society, which meant that simply being a good, loving, and responsible parent was no longer good enough.

Whether mothers have liberated themselves or not, the parents of today's teenagers have spent most of their parenting years operating under the program that was created for them by Madison Avenue executives after World War II. Whether we mothers work or stay home, we have run ourselves ragged trying to live up to the giddy standards of the mystique—doing absolutely everything for our families, being perfect wives, perfect housekeepers, and perfect mothers who must raise perfect children.

Some of the parents I see regularly I have known for many years—since our children started kindergarten together. Some of them have been parenting two, three, and more children, and some of them have been at it for as long as twenty years. They have spent their energy being intensely involved in every aspect of their children's lives, and I believe that for the most part they have spent their energy engaged in all of the more visible tasks so that, at the very least, other people wouldn't think them incompetent. Some who carried it to extremes are the mothers who were the best in their peer group—who also sewed, baked, maintained vegetable gardens, and canned their homegrown crops. The competition back then when our kids were young was pretty stiff, as it is bound to be when there exists only *one* occupation for married women to excel in.

Today when I look around at these parents who have spent so many years running around, I see a bunch of weary people, some of whom have simply burned-out and have nothing left to give at just about the most critical point in their lives as parents. Often the situation is even worse for those mothers who've been forced to return to work and yet still operate under the old traditional program.

It is very easy for the burned-out to miss the signals our youngsters send. I think now of a woman whose teenage son kept screaming at her, "You never listen to me." Of course she listened to him. When, with tears streaming down his cheeks, he railed that life was unbearable and he didn't want to live in this world, she would listen. She would even answer: "Oh, everyone feels like that once in a while. Here, take out the garbage." To "Nobody likes me; I have no friends," she would say, "Don't be silly, you have lots of friends. Here, put the plates on the table; we're running late."

And then one day the principal called and told her that she and her husband should come to the school for a conference. She said she couldn't; she worked, and why didn't he just tell her what was on his mind. She was exhausted, and she still had the laundry to do that night. If she took time off from her job to bounce over to the school every time someone thought it was a good idea, she'd have to make up the time. The principal persisted. He couldn't tell her what it was over the phone. It was very important. Critical.

So she and her husband wrenched themselves free from their jobs and met with the principal, their son's counselor, and the school psychologist. Impatiently she looked at her watch while waiting to hear about how her child's grades were slipping or that he'd cut class four times or that he and Freddie Williams had been fighting again. Instead, his face ashen, the principal told her, "We fear for your son's

life. We're not worried about his grades. This is much more important. We have been told that he's already made one attempt—with
drugs." Instantly this bone-weary, guilt-ridden mother remembered
the day a few weeks back when he'd slept a very long time and she
hadn't been able to get him to wake up and had finally dismissed it
because "teenagers sleep a lot." She also remembered him saying "I
don't want to live anymore" and "You never listen to me."

How many mothers who are locked into the exhausting patriarchal
program are able really to listen to what their children have to say?
Can they hear the very deep and searing pain in the fourteen-year-
old's voice when she says, "Nobody likes me," or "My math teacher
hates me"? Do they, for instance, ask their children why they think
that nobody likes them? Do they ask what the math teacher does and
perhaps learn that he or she singles out that child and humiliates him
in front of the other kids? Does a parent hear what a child is saying
when he or she declares that life isn't worth living? Do parents find
out if this is just a momentary mood, or an actual depression? As
pressures on teenagers mount, receptive listening from parents becomes more and more important. The suicide rate for teenagers is increasing alarmingly, and some of those teenagers are "very bright,
well behaved, and liked by both teachers and students," as it is often
reported in the newspaper after their deaths.

Sex, drugs, rock and roll, and put a ban on birth control. The explanations and solutions that we hear from the New Right are hardly
adequate to the complex problems that have been mounting for decades now.

Legacy of the Baby Boom

I tune in on Sunday at 7:00 A.M., and I become enlightened. I
learn not only that the United States of America is in danger of being
taken over by the rotten commies because we have only enough ar-
maments to kill every Russian seven times while they have enough to
kill each of us fourteen times and that depravity threatens us from
every corner, but also that permissiveness is responsible for crime in
the streets.

If you do not think too deeply about it, it makes sense. And it
makes sense, then, that a more rigid set of moral values is the obvi-

ous solution. But while permissiveness may contribute to criminal activity, it is not its cause. It is a long-established fact that the crime rate increases and decreases along with the rate of population growth in any society. Speaking to this in his book *Great Expectations* (1980), Landon Y. Jones writes:

> To see how the baby boom affected the crime rate we have to understand that America's real criminal class is not the poor or the black or the otherwise disadvantaged. Violence rather is a sport of youth. Young men especially live dangerously. The leading causes of death among the 15–24 age group, for example, are accidents, suicide, and homicide.
>
> Crime, it turns out, is almost as age-specific as driving, diapers, and dentures. Teenagers and young adults dominate crimes of violence and crimes of property. Nearly one half of all the people arrested in this country are between the ages of 14 and 24. In 1960, the 14–24 age cohort included only 15 percent of the population but accounted for 69 percent of all arrests for serious crimes. Compared to those 25 and over, the younger age group commits twice as many murders, five times as many forcible rapes, six times as many burglaries, and twenty times as many car thefts. The peak age of violent crime in the United States is 18. (Auto thieves and burglars are 16; murderers are 20.)
>
> . . . During the 1940s and the 1950s, for example, the country had enjoyed a time of relative tranquillity thanks to the low birthrates of the twenties and thirties.

In other words our current crime rate is the result of the baby-boom generation having come of age. In his book, first published in 1980, Jones predicts that as this generation gets older, we will see the crime rate drop off. On April 7, 1982, the Associated Press reported that the United States crime rate leveled off in 1981 for the first time in five years. The statistics that had been released by the FBI the day before showed that murder had dropped by three percent, aggravated assault was down two percent, motor vehicle thefts had declined by four percent, and arson had dropped by eight percent. James Fyfe of American University, an academic expert on crime, has said that he thinks the leveling off is primarily attributable to two facts: cold weather and *the aging of the American population.*

Moreover, he agrees with Jones that crimes are disproportionately committed by young people, and that the percentage of young people in the population is declining as *the baby-boom generation enters middle age.*

I would only add that we ought not to forget that one hundred percent of the inmates in San Quentin were abused as children. Child abuse, which also increases and decreases with population growth, is obviously a factor in violent crime.

Given this relationship between population growth and crime, not only is the New Right's diagnosis faulty, but what they prescribe to bring about a resurgence of morality would, in practice, lead to the greatest crime wave in the history of civilization. The procreation ethic would lead to another population explosion, the stern policies would set the stage for child abuse, and the dismantling of our welfare system would be the perfect breeding ground for runaway crime. Add to that the hateful and inflammatory rhetoric of the Evangelicals who call for such things as stoning gay people in the street and the blueprint is complete.

Secular Humanism: Another Straw Villain

It was at the conference on Public Schools and the First Amendment put on by the University of Indiana that I was witness to another demonstration of how the Religious New Right latches on to an issue of concern to parents specifically, simplistically misrepresents its causes, and then goes on to prescribe the needed solution for *all* Americans. I also had another awakening—a moment of undeniable truth—when I became aware of their hidden agenda.

Speaker after speaker pointed to literacy rates in the United States, declining test scores, and the well-publicized fact that "Johnny can't read," to make the point that public education in this country has deteriorated. Teachers in the audience squirmed in their chairs, parents (this one no exception) nodded in sad agreement. Although my children are in one of the very best school systems in the nation, the education they have thus far received (one is a senior, the other a junior in high school) is woefully deficient compared to the one I had received already by the eighth grade.

Clergymen and leaders of parent groups from all over the Midwest promised to tell us what had happened to the educational system in America and what could be done to upgrade it. And we were all ears.

Tim LaHaye, author of *The Battle for the Mind* (1980), was the first to address the question. What had gone wrong in all of society was a reflection of what had gone wrong in the public school system. Amorality and permissiveness were the values our children were being taught. These were the values of secular humanism, he told us, which was a religion being taught in the public schools. Repeatedly other speakers—Greg Dixon, Janet Egan, Terry Dodds—backed him up. The school system and our culture were going down the drain because of secular humanism.

Teachers shifted restlessly, murmuring to each other, looking questioningly at others sitting nearby: "What's secular humanism?" one asked. Another wanted to know "What's wrong with humanism?" Someone else said, "I thought humanism was a good thing—love for your fellow man and all that." A principal from a high school in Illinois stood up and protested the idea of secular humanism being taught in the public schools. "I don't even know what it is," he said. He looked embarrassed at not knowing something that apparently everyone else ought to know. Others merely looked confused.

Gradually the New Right speakers cleared up the confusion. According to Fundamentalist thought, secular humanism is a religion that promotes equality for women and homosexuals, freedom of expression, evolution, world government, sexual freedom between consenting adults, reproductive freedom of choice, and the right of individuals to make their own judgments and decisions without looking to a deity for guidance.

It is not possible *not* to teach religion, we were told. That "traditional American religion" is not being taught means that atheism, the religion of the American Humanist Association, is being taught in the schools. More evidence was offered: the teaching of evolution, which is in conflict with the biblical account of creation and is therefore unchristian and secular humanist in nature; courses such as ecology, which is anti-family in that it deals with overpopulation and necessarily with birth control. Ecology, moreover, teaches a global consciousness, thereby brainwashing schoolchildren into believing in a one-world government, which is a goal of the communist conspiracy.

The one course that seemed to come under the heaviest fire was values clarification. Dr. Murray Norris, Director of Christian Family Renewal, said that in these values clarification classes, children were often urged to keep diaries, which he feared would be read to the class or fall into the wrong hands, thus revealing personal matters that should be kept in a child's family. His major concern, however, was identical to that of Tim LaHaye and Greg Dixon, who also spoke to this issue: Values clarification teaches children that there are no absolute values of right or wrong. Instead of rigid biblical injunctions, it teaches them to think situations through, consider all relevant aspects, and then make a judgment or a decision based on their thought-out conclusions. This teaches amorality and is one of the things that is responsible for the corruption of our youth, which is a clearly defined goal of secular humanism.

According to Dr. Norris and his allies, secular humanists work to corrupt our young people through a nonchristian curriculum that promotes promiscuity, homosexuality, and general amorality in order to bring about the collapse of our divinely ordained capitalistic society from within—through the moral decay of our youth. To accomplish this they have infiltrated our school system and thrown God out of the classroom.

A goal of this "conspiracy," as I understand it, is to reduce U.S. population growth, thereby weakening our economy and our national defense system. This was explained in a very interesting manner by Greg Dixon, who told journalist Michael Disend (*Penthouse,* February 1982) that the public school system *conspires* with Planned Parenthood, SIECUS, Zero Population Growth, and the secular humanists "to create a phobia in the minds of our young people in the public schools to do away with themselves" because:

> . . . [T]hey know that to keep four billion more people from being born in nineteen years, that a certain percentage of them will have to be aborted. A certain percentage will have to be stopped through contraceptives. A certain percentage will have to be stopped through sexual satisfaction through homosexuality and lesbianism. A certain amount of people will have to be eliminated by suicide. A certain amount will have to be eliminated through sterilization. A certain amount will have to be eliminated through euthanasia. So consequently these neonazis are really teaching genocide to our young people.

It's a conscious conspiracy. They [meaning all of the groups he identified] fund their programs through abortionist centers . . . so they're trying to stir up the passions of the young people so they go out and commit fornication so the girl can get pregnant and she'll go down to the abortion center and they can get federal funds, and that's how they're funding the whole program.

The remedy to this deplorable state of affairs, according to Dixon and others, is to throw secular humanism out of the classroom and bring Christianity back into it. "It is the Christian school movement and the restoration of voluntary prayer in the public schools," Falwell tells us, "that will provide the most important means of educating our children in the concepts of patriotism and morality." To drive home his point, he quotes Republican Senator Jesse Helms:

It is hardly coincidence that the banishment of the Lord from the public schools has resulted in their being taken over by a totally Secularist philosophy. Christianity has been driven out. In its place has been enshrined a permissiveness in which the drug culture has flourished, as have pornography, crime and fornication—in short, everything but discipline and learning.

Which is why Johnny can't read.

Naturally, when these ideas were foisted on educators assembled from all over the nation, there were protests. At first some in the audience objected that no distinction was being made between those who possessed humanistic ideas—liberal thoughts—and those who were card-carrying members of the American Humanist Association. While this was not answered directly, we gradually came to understand that if you possessed even one liberal idea—if, for example, you were a member of an environmentalist organization, were opposed to the proliferation of nuclear weapons, opposed to book-burning, or opposed to capital punishment on the grounds that it was the taking of a life—that made you a secular humanist. You didn't have to pay dues to be a supporter of the movement. Another objection raised by the audience centered around bringing Christianity back into the classroom—such a move would be in violation of the First Amendment's edict of separation of church and state.

Well, wrong again, according to Greg Dixon. When the wall of separation was introduced, the purpose, he insisted, was to keep the state from interfering with the "established Christian American church" and not the other way around. Never mind that our forebears were concerned that without this wall of separation, religious freedom—*including* the freedom to practice any or no religion—would be in jeopardy.

The Real Villain

In any event, the causes of lowered performance in our public schools were stated by these zealots as absolutes. Such certainty about single, simplistic causes should arouse skepticism. As Landon Jones (1980) says, there are many influences on schoolchildren—television, nonacademic elective courses, technological changes, attitudinal changes, and myriad others that are easily identifiable enemies of literacy. Nevertheless he points out that "It is the unavoidable fact that the unprecedented size of the boom generation itself" has caused a crisis in the classroom.

The boom children appeared on the scene nearly overnight to be educated by systems that had no realistic way of planning in advance for the onslaught of their number. The once-small classroom doubled and tripled in size. In some districts it became so unmanageable that children were put on half-day sessions, which necessarily meant that they received half as much education, if that much, as some of those half-session classes were twice the size of the full-session classes we'd known before the baby-boomers hit the schools.

As one veteran teacher told me, "Suddenly there was this big need for more teachers, so we just started cranking them out. Not as adequately trained as previous generations of teachers because there were so many of them; and because they were needed fast, they were often inadequate teachers—some of them not having mastered the English language!" And, he said, the situation continues to worsen because the younger teachers are taught by professors who were inadequately taught, so poor teacher training has become nearly institutionalized into a vicious cycle. I know what he means when I find four errors in a note sent home to me by one of my children's *English* teachers.

Overcrowding compounds the problem another way—through

teacher burnout. Increased work loads, increased paperwork, and deteriorating work environments—largely the result of overcrowding—as well as unruly students all contribute to this malaise (Salter, 1982). Teachers are now adding to the list of those things that make their jobs tougher the pressure from ultraconservative parents who are distressed that children aren't being taught "traditional moral values." As one teacher I met at the Public Schools and First Amendment conference told me, "I am tired of emotionally immature parents dominating the school boards and teachers by threats." Outstanding teachers are leaving our system because this and other pressures are causing them to burn out. We can ill afford to lose good educators, but lose them we will, for the reasons cited and the fact that we don't pay them decently.

This teacher burnout also compounds the other favorite issue of the New Right—drugs. Too many baby-boom kids are moving through the system, too few teachers and other officials are there to monitor them. One teacher who is now approaching burnout told me that he is leaving because he doesn't want to get to the point a few of his colleagues have already reached: "Some of them simply look the other way when they know someone is buying or dealing because it's just one more thing to contend with, and they can't handle it. Others have said they don't really mind it if the kids smoke pot and then go to class because then at least they are docile." This is a terrible situation, of course, but before we judge too harshly the exhausted teachers who are this indifferent to drug use, we ought to try taking a walk in their shoes.

Behind "Back-to-Basics"

One answer to the problem of slipping educational standards, many parents feel, is to get students back to basics—reading, writing, and arithmetic. However, what I did not know until I attended the conference described above is that sometimes the members and leaders of the back-to-basics movements aren't simply calling for a return to the effective old methods of teaching the three R's. What unsuspecting parents may not know when they agree that it makes sense to do away with electives and nonessential curricula and focus on basic education is that the underlying agenda of New Right groups is to rid the public schools of what is perceived as humanist philosophy and replace it with religious dogma. It was at this conference that I realized that the objection to the teaching of ecology and values clarification, for example, is not really that it takes up class time that could be used for teaching reading or arithmetic. Rather it is that these courses have been identified as promoting the secular humanist philosophy.

What is truly insidious is that unsuspecting parents who do not hold the Fundamentalist view and do not know what is behind *some* of the back-to-basics movements wind up promoting the religious cause without knowing it. Worried that their children aren't getting the tools they will need in life, they agree that sex education is better left to the parents, and that values clarification, ecology, psychology, and other electives are time-consuming and should not be taught at the expense of the three R's. Such parents may later be surprised to learn that instead they will find "creation science" taught at the expense of biology.

And if they don't think about such things that much, they may not realize that creation science is a religious doctrine. Or even if they know that, they may not be aware that should this doctrine replace the theory of evolution or seriously challenge it, the teaching of science may well disappear from the public school system, simply because evolution underlies so much scientific thought. If, for example, students are taught that the earth is roughly only 10,000 years old, then they will also be required to accept the idea that the dinosaurs didn't exist millions of years ago and that fossil fuel thought to be derived from them was put into the earth by God. Numerous papers have demonstrated that the teaching of science will be in jeopardy should physics be explained away in purely religious terms. Dr. Wayne Moyer, President of the National Association of Biology Teachers, shows that the "theory" of creation cannot be *scientific* theory, as it is something that must be accepted on faith as an absolute truth. When anything must be so accepted, he told the conference, it forbids inquiry, which is what science is all about. At first glance parents may see the back-to-basics movements as nonsectarian. And then one day those same parents may wake up to realize that in their zeal to find a solution to Johnny's problems with reading, they have allowed certain groups to determine what Johnny can read once he learns how to do so. The Family Protection Act, framed and boosted by the very folks who pervert the back-to-basics movement and push religious propaganda under the guise of constitutional instruction, would make this possible:

Notwithstanding any other provision of the law, it shall be unlawful for any Federal, State, or local educational agency or institution receiving any Federal funds to—

. . . prohibit parental review of textbooks prior to their use in public school classrooms.

. . . No funds authorized under any applicable program or any provision of Federal law shall be used to secure or promote education materials or studies relating to the preparation of education materials if such materials do not reflect a balance between the status role of men and women, do not reflect different ways in which women and men live and do not contribute to the American way of life as it has been historically understood.

We know that the latter provision means that schoolchildren will be required to be taught that men are the leaders of the family and that a woman's place is in the home. What the former provision means is that each and every time an overburdened teacher wants to introduce some new teaching material, it will have to be examined by a review board or by all of the parents. What this provision also means is that if just one single parent in one district objects to material on the grounds that it doesn't teach that particular parent's brand of morality, that material can be removed. At the present time there are approximately ten cases being heard around the country that have gone to court on the strength of a small committee's or even a single parent's objection.

Helping parents decide what ought to be removed from the classroom and the school library are Mel and Norma Gabler of Texas. This lively and now famous couple are out to "cleanse the nation's schools of all materials that they consider anti-family, anti-American, and anti-God" ("This World," *San Francisco Chronicle*, August 23, 1981). Their target is textbooks. "Because of their efforts some social-studies textbooks (Jerry Falwell calls them Soviet propaganda) have been recalled, health manuals replaced, and English anthologies removed from textbook lists around the country."

The Gablers cite as their objections to these textbooks mentions of George Washington's violent temper, Watergate, and the Vietnam war. They say that we spend too much time trying to "relate and make such things relevant." So, because these materials are "negative," they would like such references to be removed from our textbooks. It should be noted that the Gablers warn parents who screen texts to insure that they are "healthy" for their children's young eyes not to read the books too carefully, as they are written very convincingly.

According to the "Special Report" section of the newsletter of People for the American Way (January 1982), the Gablers have succeeded in banning all seven social-studies textbooks up for approval in Texas this year and have purged five dictionaries from Texas schools since 1977. The newsletter quotes the Gablers as saying, "Until textbooks are changed there is no possibility that crime, violence, VD and abortion rates will do anything but continue to climb." "Instead," says the newsletter, "it is censorship cases that are skyrocketing—up five hundred percent since November 1980, according to the American Library Association."

Already this year (1982)—and the Family Protection Act, or any other similar prohibitive legislation, has yet to be passed—the ALA reports that there have been attempts to remove, restrict, or deny access to over nine hundred books that have been perceived to be in violation of the provisions of the Family Protection Act or perceived as being pornographic. The Association expects it to come close to 1,000. Here is a small sampling of the offending texts: *Working,* by Studs Terkel, *The Catcher in the Rye,* by J. D. Salinger, *The Grapes of Wrath* and *Of Mice and Men,* by John Steinbeck, *Passages,* by Gail Sheehy, *Slaughterhouse-Five,* by Kurt Vonnegut, *Little House in the Woods,* by Laura Ingalls Wilder, *1984,* by George Orwell, *Brave New World,* by Aldous Huxley, *The Adventures of Huckleberry Finn,* by Mark Twain, *The Naked Ape,* by Desmond Morris, *Best Short Stories by Negro Writers,* edited by Langston Hughes, *Soul on Ice,* by Eldridge Cleaver, *Father Christmas,* by Raymond Briggs, and *365 Days,* by Ronald Glasser.

Two of the words in *Webster's New Collegiate Dictionary* the New Right objects to are "penis" and "vagina."

Making It with Mademoiselle was also removed from some library shelves, but the Moral Majority reversed itself on learning that this is a book on dressmaking published by *Mademoiselle* magazine. This incident illustrates what was reported at the Authors' Guild meeting on February 23, 1982: Often book banners and school officials don't even read the material they remove as questionable. Avery Corman said that his book *Kramer vs. Kramer* had been removed from a reading list for high school seniors after one parent objected to it. The official didn't even bother to read it, which led Mr. Corman to conclude "It's easier to ban a book than to read it." At the same meeting, Gail Sheehy said that she had "no idea what the charges are against my book," when she learned that *Passages* had been banned.

Judith P. Krug, director of the Office of Intellectual Freedom of the American Library Association, warned:

> An atmosphere conducive to censorship hovers over the country. The trouble is not simply the present administration's tolerance of such censorial groups as the Moral Majority—it's more than just a cause-and-effect thing. Rather I really believe these censors are searching for something unreal—the good old days. It's "Alice in Wonderland" thinking. (*The New York Times,* Sept. 8, 1982.)

People for the American Way tell us that "Censorship attacks even extend to government publications on the family, which have been popular for decades." The Indiana chapter of the Moral Majority (headed by Greg Dixon) managed to pressure Senator Richard Lugar to stop automatically sending out copies of the government booklet "Your Child from One to Six" to new parents in Indiana. "The objection? The booklet advises parents not to spank their children," which "flies in the face of the Bible doctrine on discipline."

Objectionable magazines named by Cal Thomas, communications director of the Moral Majority, Inc., include *Woman's Day* (because of an article on amniocentesis), *Family Circle* (owing to Abigail Van Buren's article that suggests that homosexuals are not evil), *Redbook, Ladies' Home Journal, Good Housekeeping, McCall's,* and *Better Homes and Gardens.* As far as I can determine, these last magazines are considered subversive because they are affiliated with the others that were targeted for specific reasons. In a speech before a recent Magazine Publishers Association Conference, *People* magazine editor Richard Stolley said, "In high school libraries, the magazines most frequently singled out for attack are *Time, Newsweek, U.S. News & World Report, Psychology Today,* and *Sports Illustrated.*"

Perhaps it won't matter if Johnny can't read. If the New Right has its way, there may not be anything of any substance left to read.

Having seen New Right spokespersons in the flesh and heard them expound, I believe many are sincere. How could anyone come up with the convoluted notion of population control that Greg Dixon has and *not* be sincere? But I also believe there are those who, while *saying* that the issue of population growth is a communist-inspired one, actually see it in strictly economic terms. They may say that the only function of sexual activity is procreation, that therefore any discussion of population growth is not only secular humanist (communist) propaganda but immoral, as it leads to talk of birth control, and liberally lace what they say with mentions of God and the Bible, while in fact they are simply fronting for the corporations that will derive benefit from continued population growth.

And even though I think Mr. Dixon is sincere, after listening to him in person and reviewing the tapes of his talks at the conference I hear *fear* in his voice; and between his lines, buried in his bluster, what I hear him fearing is that the Fundamentalism he preaches will not hold up to scrutiny from students. What will happen when, for example, they are provided the opportunity to compare "creation science" to the theory of evolution and decide for themselves which notion of our beginnings makes the most sense? I hear fear when he says that values clarification and environmental education will communize our young. I hear fear that if they are taught to think for themselves or are exposed to global education, they may realize that all peoples of the world are interdependent—that we export and import goods and technology for our very survival is evidence of that. Students who see that may be obliged to recognize that Earth is the home of us all—that we need one another and therefore need to understand and respect our differing cultures, a notion that is in direct conflict with Fundamentalist isolationist teachings. That sort of realization leads students to question the wisdom of drilling for oil off the coast of California or strip mining somewhere else in the world merely because it is profitable to do so, even though it may damage the environment that belongs to us all.

Then, too, for Mr. Dixon and others in his position this holy war for the minds of American schoolchildren may have another bottom line: If a substantial percentage of Dixon's eight-thousand-member congregation loses faith, that gentleman's power would be badly eroded.

In any event, whether the motives of the various New Right leaders are based on religion or economics, when you assess their strategies—their misrepresentations of the nature of the problems of our young people; their simplistic and childish explanations of these problems (God has moved out of the classroom and mother has unchained herself from the stove); their stated goal of religious indoctrination from kindergarten through college; their censorship of materials that can be perceived as subversive only insofar as they stimulate free thought—what these groups are attempting seems to be mind control.

In the same way that the hierarchies of ultraconservative religious denominations have brainwashed their women into submission and into working to maintain their own oppression, these leaders now wish to reach others outside of their spheres of reference—you and me, whether we are Christians or Jews, Protestants or Catholics, Buddhists or atheists, and brainwash new generations of American children to turn away from the faiths of their *own* fathers and mothers and join the true faith as the New Right sees it.

Their way is the *only* way.

Sex, drugs, rock and roll. Now it's time for mind control.

VII

IT CAN NEVER HAPPEN
IN AMERICA

Need we ask why we cannot forget about authoritarian religion and concentrate upon the problem of a good life in a good world? We are not allowed to. Reactionary forces are at work among us—well-organized forces—often under the leadership of able, high-minded and sincere persons, and they are seeking to take advantage of the present sense of confusion and uncertainty to fasten the grip of a supreme authority in the name of God over the whole of human life, although these forces reflect an outgrown stage in man's intellectual and spiritual evolution.

Max Otto

A Chilling Echo

Many ominous trends surfaced at that 1982 conference on the Public Schools and the First Amendment. On the morning of the second session, when Bishop James Armstrong (United Methodist Church), Rabbi Jonathan Stein (Indianapolis Hebrew Congregation), Father Donald L. Schmidling (St. Joan of Arc), and Greg Dixon were gathered together on a panel to discuss the question "Should religion have a role in the public schools?", the agenda behind the New Right movement became clearer to me.

All but Dixon agreed that religion should be taught in the schools as part of an overall course on religion and the history of Western

civilization. Dixon maintained that religion was already being taught
in the public schools—amoral religion—and that the "faith of our fathers" should be restored to the classroom. He harped, he railed, he
repeated that nonchristian evolution, sex education, and pornography, the promotion of perversion, were permeating our public classrooms. Secular humanism, secular humanism, secular humanism.
The only time in my memory that I have ever heard one person use
the same phrase so many times in such a short space of time was
when my son was four years old and said, "Mommy gimme, Mommy
gimme, Mommy gimme," whenever he wanted something passionately.

Finally Rabbi Stein confronted the real issue. All of this talk about
secular humanism for two solid days, he said, was simply a device
to "rally the troops by identifying the enemy."

There was stunned silence in the conference hall as the weight of
these words, spoken by a descendant of scapegoats in another time,
sunk in. The implications hit me in a wave. In one moment I realized
that the Nazis had gone after the Jews because Jews have been
taught down through the ages to think for themselves, to reason, to
weigh the different sides of a premise—to question, question, question. Had they had the chance, the Jews in Nazi Germany would
have *questioned* what was going on, so they had to be identified as
the enemy of the people and gotten rid of before they caused other
Germans to question. Jews are the original practitioners of the values
clarification so hated by the New Right for one reason alone—it
teaches children how to think, to ask questions. "Christians, like soldiers and slaves, ask no questions," says Jerry Falwell.

I went to that conference to understand—to lessen my rage through
tolerance and understanding of a different point of view. I had agreed
with the mayor of Indianapolis when he had opened the conference
saying that this was a historic event—a wonderful occasion—when
people of differing opinions had come together to reason. But I
walked out of those conference halls chilled to the bone at the paral-
lels between the Religious New Right and the greatest mind-con-
trollers of all time.

Among the first of Adolf Hitler's acts when he came into power
in Germany were the banning of abortion and the shutting down of
birth-control clinics. And, as is true of the New Right, he advocated
—successfully—outlawing homosexuality, quelling the rising women's

liberation movement in that country, and establishing the patriarchal family as "the basic unit." His words, Jerry Falwell's words, Tim LaHaye's words, Greg Dixon's words, and the words of Howard Phillips, member of the Board of Directors of the Moral Majority. The words of them *all*. "The basic unit." In *Mein Kampf,* Hitler wrote some other words that are part of the New Right rhetoric:

> Her world is her husband, her family, her children and home. We do not find it right when a woman presses into the world of men. Rather we find it natural when these two worlds remain separate. . . . Woman and man represent two quite different types of being. Reason is dominant in man.

Of the time just prior to Hitler's takeover in Germany, Richard Evans, author of *The Feminist Movement in Germany—1894–1933,* writes that there existed a view among conservatives in that nation that

> . . . The women's movement was . . . destroying the family . . . by encouraging married women to take jobs, by supporting unmarried mothers, and by urging women in general to be more independent. It was endangering Germany's military potential by discouraging marriage (encouraging family planning and thus lowering the birthrate). It was outraging nature by campaigning for the systematic equalization of the sexes and by inciting women to do things they were unsuited for. It was international in spirit and unpatriotic.

Joseph Paul Goebbels could have written Falwell's lines for him:

> When we eliminate women from public life, it is not because we want to dispense with them, but because we want to give them back their essential honor. . . . The outstanding and highest calling of women is always that of wife and mother. (Lucy Komisar, *The New Feminism,* 1972.)

Whether by design or accident, the "Nazi Connection" is very clear-cut. In her piece of that title (1982), Gloria Steinem writes of the stunning similarities in the premises and the tactics of the New Right and Hitler's regime, and of the similarities between the times that allowed a Hitler to happen and the climate of the eighties. In a very detailed account she describes the women's movement in Germany as being nearly identical to the movement in this country today. The economic situation was similar to ours, as was the low morale from having been defeated in World War I.

In their well-researched and thoroughly documented book *Holy Terror* (1982), Flo Conway and Jim Siegelman buttress Steinem's observations:

> In their most blatant instances, some fundamentalist right campaigns follow the historical lead of the propaganda machine assembled in Nazi Germany. Like the current movement, that deadly regime aspired to power in a time of economic crisis and public reaction to social change. . . .
>
> . . . In the aftermath of Germany's humiliating defeat, Hitler entered politics and began to formulate a strategy he described as "spiritual terror." In 1920, he adopted the "hooked cross" or swastika as his emblem, coupling popular Aryan myths with the rampant anti-Semitism of the era. He condemned "democracy and humanism" and fumed over the moral decay of German society. In later writings, Hitler railed at length over the horrors of syphilis in tones foreshadowing modern-day fundamentalists.

No one is suggesting that the New Right is part of some covert Nazi conspiracy, but the similarities between the dogmas, strategies, and tactics are stunning. A loose connection between old-line ultraconservatives—the Nazis—and Phyllis Schlafly, who speaks Hitler's lines when she talks about women's roles, is not out of the question, either.

For instance, in 1941 Clarence Manion, who founded the Manion Forum, an organization that has funded Phyllis Schlafly's right-wing activities for a number of years, became a member of the National Committee of the America First Committee. The Committee was led by General Robert E. Wood, then Chairman of the Board of Sears, Roebuck and Co. This was an isolationist organization that was "evidently shown to be infiltrated by elements opposed to American efforts to stop Hitler's march in Europe," according to Arnold Forster and Benjamin R. Epstein, authors of *Danger on the Right* (1976). At the time Manion joined it, America First was arguing that the United States should turn its back on Europe's problem. "Such an attitude," say Forster and Epstein, "made it obvious that pro-Nazis would quickly try to insinuate themselves into the organization, and these isolationists apparently did nothing to stop their infiltration."

The America First Committee was funded by the Lilly Endowment Foundation of Indianapolis. What caught my attention was that the conference I attended that provided a forum for right-wing views was cosponsored by the Intercollegiate Society for Individualists, which is also funded by the Lilly Endowment Foundation.

Whether or not these affiliations are significant, the American New Right shares with the Nazi party the goal of overthrowing our democratic government. They say as much in their own literature. The idea is so outrageous that some people find it difficult to accept. But one has only to read Tim LaHaye's book *The Battle for the Mind* (1980), which asserts that any school system that advocates freedom of thought—*freedom of thought*—is bent on brainwashing our children. Such doublespeak, distortion, and out-and-out untruths are standard operating procedure for LaHaye and his fellow travelers.

"After concluding that the intelligence of the masses was very limited, Hitler then developed his notion of the principle of the 'big lie'" (Conway and Siegelman, 1982). That is, an enormous lie with just a kernel of truth—so big that people would not believe it to be a lie because they themselves may lie about small things but would be ashamed of lies that were too big. One big lie: Secular humanism is part of a communist conspiracy to destroy the United States; it is a religion being taught in our public schools. Since many humanistic issues are currently being discussed in our public schools, there's just enough truth to this for those with limited intelligence or those who are brainwashed to believe this. Other big lies: Feminism is responsible for the breakdown of the American family and promiscuity. Established literary works are pure smut and pornographic (that is, they stimulate thought). The New Right, however, does not confine itself to just big lies but has developed a practiced art—a near reflex—of putting out little factual inaccuracies.

For example, in his book *The Battle for the Mind,* in addition to the distorted right-wing rhetoric about secular humanism and feminism, LaHaye makes a certain point by saying that Brazil and Australia are larger than the United States, when they are not. He says that because of socialism Sweden has the highest suicide rate in the world. It has not. He says that humanists want the United States to merge with the Soviet Union, while humanists (Andrei Sakharov, for example) are thrown in jail there. He also says that the ERA was not favored in any polls. What polls? His? Among his congregation, who follow like sheep? Finally he says, as a statement of absolute fact, that the signatories of an ad in *The New York Times* calling for a one-world government comprised "the Who's Who of humanism." Well, I was one of the signatories, and while I consider myself to be a humanitarian, I have never been a member of the Humanist Association. Nor to my knowledge were most of the other signers of the ad.

Inroads on Our Freedom

Anyone with any doubts that the goal of the New Right is to turn our nation into a Fundamentalist Christian state should review their agenda. As to their capability of doing so, the book *Holy Terror* makes an alarming assessment:

> As we assembled the parts of the fundamentalist-right model, its driving myths, controlling techniques and almost magical dependence on new media technology, we had no trouble drawing parallels to major propaganda systems of the twentieth century. But those parallels soon ran askew. . . . In our society, with its built-in checks and balances, its broad accepted individual freedoms and its diversity of competing voices, not one of these accepted practices, nor all of them together, comprise anything close to a system of total propaganda, that is, a comprehensive attack on the thoughts, feelings, beliefs, values and guiding vision of a people and their culture—culminating in the outright seizure of power. In that sense, Americans have never experienced total propaganda the way people have in Germany, Russia, China and other nations.
>
> Until now. In our view, the assault on secular society by the fundamentalist right constitutes such a threat. It is the first instance of total propaganda brought home to the United States.
> . . . The fundamentalist-right model may be the most comprehensive of all, comprising the classic elements of total propaganda: a mammoth mass-communications network, a tightly coordinated political machine, a fiercely independent education

system—all predicated, for the first time, on the deep structure of religion and suffused to grass-roots levels through a coalescence of separatist churches, Bible studies, parachurch and missionary organizations. Its expressed objectives, as fundamentalist-right spokesmen have described them . . . [are] to Christianize the nation, to fill all government positions with "Bible-believing" Christians, to gain ascendancy over the national media, to have fundamentalist beliefs taught as science in public schools, to dictate the meaning of human life and, ultimately, to convert every person on earth. (Conway and Siegelman, 1982.)

To convert every person on earth.

In reviewing the progress that has been made to date, Conway and Siegelman pinpoint the events of 1978, when the politics of apathy, religion, and reaction against liberalism added a new cadre of zealots to the existing one in our Senate. Senators Jake Garn and Orrin Hatch of Utah, Paul Laxalt of Nevada, James McClure of Idaho, millionaire rancher Malcolm Wallop of Wyoming; representatives Philip Crane of Illinois, Robert Dornan of California, Mickey Edwards of Oklahoma, and Larry McDonald of Georgia were that year joined by: the new senators Gordon Humphrey of New Hampshire, Roger Jepsen of Iowa, William Armstrong of Colorado, John Warner of Virginia, and Phil Gramm of Texas.

By 1979, Conway and Siegelman tell us, "movement loyalists had found key positions on Senate committees such as Budget, Banking, and Labor and Human Resources, and established a strong presence in a number of equally powerful House Committees and Subcommittees."

And then came the sweep in 1980 with the election of former film star Ronald Reagan costumed in mainline conservatism that masked his deep ties to the far right. His success not only ushered in a platform of absolute Fundamentalism (wholesomely espoused in nice-guy fashion), but another cadre of zealots, including senators Jeremiah Denton of Alabama, Don Nickles of Oklahoma, Dan Quayle of Indiana, Charles Grassley of Iowa, Steven Symms of Idaho, James Abdnor of South Dakota, Bob Kasten of Wisconsin, and Paula Hawkins of Florida.

An infusion of money into New Right activities from corporate interests and brainwashed followers accompanied the formation of a network of powerful organizations such as the Moral Majority, Inc., the National Conservative Political Action Committee, the Conservative Caucus, the Committee for the Survival of a Free Congress, the National Right-to-Life Committee, Stop ERA, and dozens of other political, educational, and research organizations.

Spearheaded by Paul Weyrich, head of Heritage Foundation, an organizational genius who pulled the various organizations together because of their support for the same issues, this new movement was promoted (and funded too) by direct-mail wizard Richard A. Viguerie. Legend has it that Viguerie hand-copied the names of Barry Goldwater's contributors after working with Goldwater and parlayed that list into one with the names of millions of people who support right-wing causes—everyone from those who oppose gun control to those who support anti-choice legislation. Ultimately they wound up with a well-financed and well-oiled piece of political machinery.

Then they loaded up this new weapon with fear and aimed it at a gullible constituency. For those of you who weren't on the mailing list, here is a sample of the sorts of mailings that were sent out.

THIS LETTER WILL MAKE YOU ANGRY!

But I'm Going to Tell
You the Truth About . . .
        . . . Militant Gays
        . . . Liberal Educators
        . . . Cruel Atheists
        . . . and Godless Politicians

Dear friend:

I am rushing you this urgent letter because the children in
your neighborhood are in danger.

How would you feel if tomorrow your child . . .
        . . . was taught by a practicing homosexual?
        . . . was bused 20 to 30 miles away to school every morning?
        . . . was forced to attend classes in a school where all religion is banned?
If you think this could never happen . . .
        . . . you are in for a shock.

Whether any of the allegations in the letter were close to the truth or not—it scared people. These sort of fear mailings were used along with commercials that advertised pro-choice or liberal incumbents as "baby killers." In 1980 the elections really were not so much *for* specific candidates as *against* incumbents. And when the elections were actually for specific candidates, those candidates were hand-picked by the New Right. Fear and ignorance proved to be exploitable qualities. Jerry Falwell got two million Fundamentalists, who had never before bothered to exercise their right and their duty to register and vote, to vote for the first time—the way he and his henchmen told them to.

All this could happen because some of us didn't bother to vote. And because some of us didn't believe it could. It happened because some of us did not look past the slogans and the homilies and the promises to reduce our income taxes. It happened because some of us didn't stop to think about the fact that just because New Right spokespersons said they were pro-family didn't necessarily mean they were. It happened because some of us believe, in knee-jerk fashion, that religious men (or those who say they are) are necessarily "good," and that anyone who waves the Bible around couldn't be an out-and-out opportunistic liar.

Because this movement succeeded, a piece of legislation that denies poor women access to safe abortion has passed, one that might deny it to all women may pass, teenagers may soon be denied access to birth control, and battered children may be left unprotected by the law.

The Executive Connection

Meanwhile, back at the ranch in California or at his White House in Washington, D.C., the President of the United States, the keeper of the public trust, has done his part on behalf of the New Right since he took office. After the sweep in 1980 Ronald Reagan's ties to the Fundamentalist fringe were reflected by his early governmental appointments: Dr. C. Everett Koop, a Fundamentalist who is passionately anti-choice, became our Surgeon General; Marjory E. Mecklenburg, president of one of the nation's largest anti-abortion committees, was named director of the Office of Adolescent Pregnancy Programs; Robert Billings, former executive director of the Moral Majority, became "consultant and assistant" to the Secretary of Education, and later was promoted to a $50,000-a-year post as director of the Education Department's ten regional offices and as special "Christian school liaison officer" (a newly created position for which no counterpart exists for other religious denominations); former editor of Richard Viguerie's *New Right Report,* Morton C. Blackwell, became the White House Religious Affairs Director; and, of course, James Watt—a member of the Assemblies of God, a man with ties to Joseph Coors, Chevron, and Exxon, who favors selling our parks and preserves to private industrialists and supports offshore drilling at whatever cost—was appointed as Secretary of the Interior. Talk about the fox guarding the chicken coop.

Ronald Reagan's deep alliance with the Religious New Right is there to see for anyone who reads a newspaper. He doesn't always make the puppeteers happy, but when that's the case, he's quick to do a mea culpa of sorts, as evidenced by his telephoning Jerry Falwell to reassure him, after her appointment to the United States Supreme Court, that Sandra Day O'Connor was right on all "our" issues. Perhaps what really mollified Falwell was the evidence that Reagan is not only pushing for the New Right's prayer amendment, he is also pushing to dilute the courts, a goal of the New Right because the courts can make laws or overturn laws if they find them unconstitutional—a democratic door the New Right would like to nail shut. Glaring evidence of the alliance with the New Right and the willingness to disrupt our system of checks and balances is contained in one very small paragraph in a *New York Times* story on Reagan and school prayer:

> "Well, obviously the purpose of the Constitutional amendment is to circumvent the Supreme Court and to put it (the prayer issue) out of their reach," said Falwell, who was invited to the White House for the announcement. . . .

Another powerful way in which Ronald Reagan has helped to orchestrate the right-wing conspiracy to take over our nation is his use of the media:

> . . . [I]n his own way and from within the nation's highest office, working in concert with the entire fundamentalist right network, in our view, President Reagan is conducting a flagrant campaign of Holy Terror against the American public.

. . . [I]n his first year in office, he repeatedly took advantage of his unique access to the media, mounting broad-based propaganda offensives which relied heavily on indirect means of manipulating public opinion, congressional legislation and other integral functions of the democratic process. . . . The Reagan strategy combines, for the first time by an American President, the bold use of overt political propaganda carried out in unofficial cooperation with extra-governmental forces. Foremost among those forces is the vast propaganda network of the fundamentalist right, including leading elements of the electronic church and the new right's direct-mail, direct-phone and other high-technology channels. (Conway and Siegelman, 1982.)

He helps them, they help him, and he and they are one. While Ronald Reagan promotes right-wing dogma cloaked in Americana on ABC, CBS, and NBC, Jerry Falwell never misses the opportunity to run a little film clip to show the faithful followers of *The Old Time Gospel Hour* how their president is supporting their causes.

In addition to Reagan's "unique access" to the mass media, which enables him to reach the as-yet unconverted, all of the mailings sent out on his behalf, and all of the mailings sent out on his letterhead in support of right-wing candidates, there are the Christian broadcasting channels. These are both well equipped and extremely well funded. Pat Robertson's brainchild, Christian Broadcasting Network, is making inroads to the unconverted through two shows aimed at the general public. One is a soap opera that is loaded with Christian brainwashing, and the other is the talk show *The 700 Club,* which is syndicated and on which numerous popular guests (Pat Boone, for example) and the authors of books written for the popular audience appear.

Philip Zimbardo, my coauthor on an earlier book, was once a guest on *The 700 Club*. He returned from his interview absolutely flabbergasted by the facilities of this network. "It was the most sophisticated setup I've ever seen in my life," said Zimbardo, who has appeared on hundreds of other TV shows and been in as many studios. "Satellites, incredible broadcasting range, computers, the works. Obviously lots of money behind it. It puts the three big networks combined to shame. If Jim Jones had had this setup, he could have taken over the world."

The Danger Ahead

Sometimes spokesmen for the New Right make statements that are laughable. But it would be a serious, perhaps democratically fatal, mistake to laugh them off. As Harry Truman would say, history is our greatest teacher. To think that because the New Right is absurd they will not be successful demonstrates that we do not remember, for example, Prohibition. Fanatical Fundamentalists had tried to push this for over a hundred years. In *The Great Illusion* (1950), Herbert Asbury says that they'd been around and been behaving so ridiculously for so long that few sensible people took them seriously. And then one day Americans woke up and discovered that the "drys" had been victorious. And both the "wets" and the "drys" soon learned that the great morality that was promised never came, but instead bootleggers, moonshiners, rumrunners, hijackers, gangsters, racketeers, trigger men, venal judges, corrupt police, crooked politicians, and speakeasy operators—and blindness from the bad liquor that was made to replace that which had been safe for human consumption, and the perfect opportunity for organized crime to gain a foothold that would allow it to flourish. As Asbury put it, the moralists of the day were met with all manner of low life, "all bearing the twin symbols of the Eighteenth Amendment—the tommy gun and the poisoned cup."

However absurd the agenda of the far right was then, and however hidden from view the possible negative consequences of legislated morality may have been back then, the old agenda was ever apparent for a very long time. The *new* agenda of the *New* Right is just as apparent, and both it and its consequences are there for anyone with ears to hear or eyes to read. The New Right wishes to deprive women of all of their rights as a step toward overthrowing our present form of government. Women have been targeted. Should ultraconservatives gain control of our Congress, they would have good reason not to stop at the issues of equality or freedom of choice but instead go all the way back to depriving us of our right to vote. It is stated very well by William Greider in *Rolling Stone* (August 19, 1982):

> Collectively, given all their discontents and desires, women are becoming the new antiestablishment force in politics. And they have a natural advantage that outsiders assaulting the established order lack: women are the voting majority.
>
> The best evidence that something deep is happening comes from attitudes of working women, particularly younger ones. Working women, now the majority of all women, express the views most divergent from men. As more and more women enter the job market in this decade, they will have a bread-and-butter stake in political decisions and a direct basis for their own independent opinions. When one survey in 1981 asked citizens for their party identification, men chose the Democratic party over the Republican by a margin of ten percentage points. Women chose the Democratic party by a margin of twenty-one percent. Working women, however, favored the Democrats by twenty-nine percent.

Furthermore, *The New York Times*/CBS News Polls, taken in 1980, show that nearly *twice* as many women are Democrats as are Republicans (forty-one percent as opposed to twenty-three percent, with eleven percent calling themselves Independents). (It is my guess that most Republican women would not be of the radical stripe, but instead moderate.)

The Democratic party definitely cannot shape an administration under which the New Right plan can flourish for any length of time. A handy way to get rid of it, once there is a majority of fascists in the Senate and the House, is to rescind the rights of the voting majority. Paranoia? We are talking about, remember, a band of psychological terrorists who are adamantly opposed to equality for women and adamantly opposed to women maintaining jurisdiction over their own bodies, the leaders of which have stated that they will stop at nothing to get their way.

As long as women continue to exercise their rights, it will be uphill for the impatient New Right. Laws to keep women barefoot and pregnant can be seen as a means of keeping them ill-informed in their busy and lowly places.

Certain alarming signs indicate that the New Right may actually be successful in the not-too-distant future. The first is that all of the various right-wing organizations are now pulling together. There is also the not-often-talked-about alliance that has been formed with the Mormon Church. In the past, Fundamentalists traditionally disapproved of Mormonism and anyone who practiced it because Mormonism is based on the Book of Mormon and not on the rigid literal interpretation of the Scriptures. But they seem to have set aside this bias in light of the fact that Mormons and Fundamentalists have nearly identical goals for women. Currently there are more links than differences in their doctrines. All of the various ultraconservative religious denominations have very deep ties to the John Birch Society. A more recent link is that Fundamentalists, ultraconservative Catholics, and Mormons have made common cause in an organization that purports to be neither religious nor political, but one that exists to uphold the United States Constitution. This is the Freemen Institute, founded by W. Cleon Skousan, a Utah Mormon who reportedly was the mentor of United States Senator Orrin Hatch. According to an account in the *Philadelphia Inquirer* (July 5, 1981), Skousan has a strong ally in Jerry Falwell; members of the Moral Majority take part in the Freemen Institute's programs and seminars.

The alliance between Fundamentalists and Mormons promises to be a very strong one, and one to which we must all pay close attention. However, some (individual) Mormons believe that the Fundamentalists have downplayed ideological differences to gain the support of the powerful and wealthy Mormon organization. One Mormon woman who has been keeping her eye on this recent marriage believes that in the interests of their biblical absolutist values, the Fundamentalists will actually turn on the Church of the Latter-Day Saints once the purpose of their support has been served and the Fundamentalists no longer need them. If she is correct, the power play that could ensue would prove most interesting.

Another sign that they could achieve their goals has to do with what is called "the swing vote." As described in *Holy Terror,* it is that margin by which an incumbent Congressman or Senator is reelected to public office. If his margin is not very great, say, if it is only seven percent, and he perceives that seven percent to be anti-choice, he is not going to vote against anti-choice legislation. In California, even though the majority of Californians are pro-choice, all who are, are not necessarily pro-Senator Cranston. I believe this is the reason why lame-duck Senator Hayakawa has consistently voted against anti-choice proposals in the Congress, while his Democratic colleague, on the other hand—who wishes to remain in office—manages to be absent when these bills come to a vote. One has nothing to lose, the other has his seat at stake, or perhaps fears that he does. One incumbent described in *Holy Terror* is not anti-choice, but he has consistently voted anti-choice on the legislation as it comes up because he fears the loss of that seven percent of the voters that he needs to return him to office.

Also on the side of the New Right is voter apathy. Many of the women who are nominally opposed to restrictive abortion laws, including those who have had abortions themselves, are so young they do not remember a time when women were unable to obtain abortions on request. Thus they have no real sense that this is an issue that warrants their attention. What has always been there for them will always be. Sometimes they vote, sometimes they don't. Some who have never had an abortion doubt that such legislation could ever pass and even if it did, they don't anticipate an unwanted pregnancy. And some women who've terminated a pregnancy vow they will never be in that position again. It is an attitude of "What's this got to do with me?" Even among those who believe that some day women might be denied reproductive freedom of choice, all too often I hear from those who are reasonably affluent, "Well, if it comes to that and I need an abortion, I'll just go to Japan." (Or Sweden, etc.)

If such people could think sufficiently beyond their own situations, they could help to protect their own democratic freedoms in a much broader way. My own "altruism" is selfish. While it is very doubtful that anti-choice legislation would affect me personally, and while the ERA's passage has nothing to do with my particular line of work, I know that the deprivation of these rights can lead to the deprivation of my other rights—and, of course, those of my daughter.

Fundamentalist Christianity discourages all inquiry (including scientific), creativity, and originality in literature and the arts (yes, they would tell the artist what he or she can and cannot paint), and virtually all intellectual pursuits. Should it fully invade our classrooms and other institutions and cause those of us who believe differently to be intimidated, we will see the death of the human spirit. The human spirit is a gift from God—one that some of us never use, but one that some of us cherish as life itself. What this would mean is well put by the late psychiatrist Robert Lindner in his book *Must You Conform?* (1956):

> In the time of their demise, it has been characteristic of all peoples that they have surrendered to pressures put upon them by their power-mad leaders, by their insane religions and by their misguided philosophies to conform. Protest becomes outlawed, submission the chief of virtues, and the expression of individuality by word or act a cardinal sin. But because it is not the nature of man to submit, an intolerable tension arises within him. Forced from without to conform and from within to rebel, he makes a compromise: he rebels within the limits set up by the social order he has not permitted to be erected around him. Just so does he become transformed into a storm trooper, N.K.V.D. inquisitor, guard on the long march from Corregidor, or burner of the fiery cross. And just so is the world he makes transformed into an immense Dachau.

For some reason I think of all of the true believers or the brainwashed or whatever you want to call them, and I think that they, in their own way, are rebelling within the limits of conformity. Were I not terrified of their treachery, I would weep for their misery. And, yes, possibly pray for their souls.

VIII

WITH THE BRAINS
GOD GAVE YOU . . .

Democracy is essentially antiauthoritarian—that is, it not only demands the right but imposes the responsibility of thinking for ourselves.

Bergen Evans

The Need for Vigilance

Think.

To vote intelligently one does not have to spend months and months researching the issues and taking them apart—but one does have to *think* and be wary of nice-sounding slogans and simple solutions to complex problems. Be aware, for example, that the pious religious leader or legislator who rails about fornication, perversion, communism, godless humanism, pornography, illicit sex, and morality isn't necessarily moral or ethical himself.

In California we were given a stunning example of this in State Senator John Schmitz, a self-righteous Catholic and the father of seven children. Schmitz, who when he threw his hat in the ring for the United States Senate stated that he was the "perfect Moral Majority candidate," has railed with the best of them about "illicit sex" and has introduced a record number of chastity and anti-choice pieces of legislation. But in July of 1982 it was revealed that the very married Schmitz was the father of two illegitimate children born to his mistress of some years' standing. The story broke when one of the children, a thirteen-month-old boy, was taken to the hospital for treatment for having had hair wound around his penis so tightly that it was nearly severed and required reconstructive surgery. As the saga continued Schmitz's girl friend was arrested for child abuse. Later additions to the story: Schmitz, like most right wingers, is opposed to federal support of child-abuse prevention centers and one of his *legitimate* grown sons is the godfather of Schmitz's out-of-wedlock son.

Beware of the pious. When a Jesse Helms or an Orrin Hatch or a Henry Hyde promises a return to morality and a reduction in premarital sex by legislating against the "murder of innocents," remember to move your eyes down to the bottom line and see what the consequences of such legislation might be for the pregnant cancer victim who would be denied therapy; look at the potential consequences for any living children she might already have. And then take a walk in her shoes.

And when Mr. Reagan, along with his buddy Senator Paul Laxalt, who introduced the Family Protection Act, laments the decline of the family because of the divorce rate, please keep it in mind that both of these gentlemen are divorced, the former's daughter is on her fourth marriage, and the latter's recent divorce was a messy affair.

When Phyllis Schlafly says that women already have equality under the law, think for a moment and recall those 1,600 laws on our books that discriminate against women.

When someone like James Watt says that a liberal incumbent governor who is running for a seat in the United States Senate is responsible for the state of California having granted "hundreds of permits" for off-shore drilling despite that governor's stated position against this activity, ask some questions. Mr. Watt may be mistaken. In fact, he was when he "thanked" Jerry Brown for issuing all of those permits. Watt failed to mention that only ten such permits had been issued since 1969 and they were all on existing leases. But then Brown was running against Pete Wilson, a conservative Republican and one of the new darlings of the New Right.

And when Moral Majoritarians like Jerry Falwell, Tim LaHaye, and John ("Terry") Dolan rant and rave about "sexual perversion" such as homosexuality, you need to know that, according to one of his lovers, one of the trio is himself a practicing homosexual.

In *God's Bullies: Power Politics and Religious Tyranny* author Perry Deane Young reports on a homosexual relationship between Terry Dolan, leader of the National Conservative Political Action Committee, and another man. The Committee's unstinting attacks on other gays illustrates rather beautifully Dolan's statements that anything—be it lying, cheating, or inciting the blind followers to violence—goes if it serves the New Right cause.

If, despite such hypocrisy, you are still tempted to believe that denying homosexuals equality under the law and driving them back into the closet will protect our children from "amorality" and "molestation," remember that many perverts who *do* molest children consider themselves to be "respectable heterosexuals" and are often quite moralistic. The practice of stigmatizing homosexuals, which historically, if invisibly, has caused great pain and ripped families and individuals apart, may well underlie some of the very problems that at least a few of our young people experience.

For instance, a woman I grew up with was reared in a very rigid Baptist home. Sexual repression and obsession was the name of the family game. At fifteen this woman's sister was thought to be a nymphomaniac, which is one response to having been reared in a sick environment. My friend, whom I will call Jill, was most chaste. At nineteen she married one of the more eligible men in our social group and, after a decent interval, gave birth to a baby girl. Two years after her child was born, she and Mr. Wonderful divorced. It was after that that Jill made passes first at her best friend and then at me. Her best friend was shocked, and although I was, too, I stuck around long enough to ask, "What's going on here?" The dam burst: Jill told me that she'd always known that she preferred females and that she'd married to hide her "ugly and sinful" secret. Move the frames two years ahead and we see the ex-husband, once named "the boy most likely to succeed," in his alcoholic stupor. Advance the frames another eleven years and take a look at the daughter who was a product of this unfortunate marriage: at thirteen baby girl Elizabeth is a drug addict who has already had two abortions.

A less tragic story is George's, though not by much. George was my hairstylist for a number of years, during the course of which he told me that he was gay and felt that he had had to hide this fact of his life from his religious parents, relatives, and friends, or risk being ostracized. "So I married a wonderful girl. I drank a lot because it was expected that I perform in bed. Well, I performed well enough so that we had two kids." And then George met Charles. They fell in love and decided to leave their Bible-Belt community and go to San Francisco. "When I walked out of the house and down the road, I looked back and saw my wife standing at the window with the kids. She was sobbing. She was calling to me to come back—not to leave them." One could easily indict George for leaving his wife, but before we do that, we'd do well to indict a society that pressured George to run for cover at the expense of "a wonderful girl" and two children. Naturally the "wonderful girl" became a single mother, totally responsible for the care of two children.

Finally I spoke to a woman who had been married for thirty years to a man she learned was homosexual. She married not just in church, but in good faith. She told me, "My second child had just been born and I was putting away my husband's clean socks when I saw some letters. I was foolish. I couldn't resist the temptation to read them. I nearly passed out when I read about this torrid affair my husband was having with a man. I went berserk. I wanted to kill my babies, and kill myself. I dwelled in the house of pain for years. I cannot tell you how much something like this hurts. I'd loved him so much, was committed for life. I recovered from the shock enough to go on. I was a housewife and totally dependent on him for support. I was trapped."

These marriages made in hell could be multiplied in the future in the climate created by the Religious New Right. For those who have been pressured by society to marry and hide their homosexuality, the toll in human suffering is something we will never fully know. This sort of social pressure is *hardly* the way to preserve the American family.

According to numerous reports, not only does the Moral Majority and Company advocate depriving homosexuals of their rights as citizens, some members of the group advocate depriving them of their rights to exist. Dean Wyckoff, for example, who is head of the Santa Clara County Moral Majority, told a reporter ("This World," *San Francisco Chronicle,* July 5, 1981) that homosexuality is "one of those sins that could be coupled with murder, that it would be the government that sits upon this land that would be executing homosexuals."

In thinking of the consequences of sending gay people—possibly to save their own skins—back into the matrimonial closet, ask yourself the bigot's question: "But would you want your sister/daughter/brother/son to *marry* one?"

Cultural Programming

That homosexuals do marry because of the social pressure put upon them to give at least the illusion of being like everyone else raises the whole issue of the merit of conforming for the sake of conformity and, strangely, raises many questions that apply to us all. How many of us have made important life decisions on the basis of conformity instead of on the basis of thoughtful consideration?

How many of us have—especially in the past—married because of social pressure? How many of us planned our families wisely? How many parents who practice family planning think very deeply about parenthood? How many think beyond what it might be like to have a baby, to what an awesome responsibility having children might be? How many today are caught up in the new "pregnancy chic," unaware that their desire to have children may be the result of media manipulation?

I look at the Religious New Right and I see a bunch of fanatics who would force others into parenthood by law but yet are unwilling to bear any responsibility for the children who would be born as a result. And then I look at the media and find that once again they have made common cause with the New Right by fostering nearly the same procreation ethic but with a bit more glitter. The message from either camp is: "Have babies."

A good example of how effective this current wave of cultural programming really is can be seen in the lament of one woman who was interviewed by June Adams for a piece in *McCall's Working Mother*. She explained that she and her husband worked different hours.

> We have from six at night, when my husband gets home, until ten, when I have to get ready to leave. Three of those hours are for the kids—dinner, playtime, bath. My husband wants to make love when I have to be at work or, worse, when I come home in

the morning after working all night. The only time we have sex is on Saturday mornings—*if* our toddler sleeps until eight. Our love life is practically nonexistent. We want another child, but I don't know where we're going to find the time to even conceive one!

Family planning! This woman's major complaint is that she doesn't have enough time with her husband. Another child will give her more? If she barely has the time to *conceive* another child, where does she think she's going to find the time to take care of one?

But then the poor woman probably cannot turn on the television set nor pick up a magazine without having the baby-sell hit her between the eyes. When *Time* magazine cheers on "The New Baby Bloom," as it did on February 22, 1982, we know that having babies is big news, and that everyone is doing it. Wonderful, glorious. Even couples who are old enough to be grandparents and already have very full lives are doing it. When, for example, a well-known reporter had a child at forty—her husband was sixty—did they realize that when that baby reaches eighteen, his father will be seventy-eight years old—if he lives that long?

But those who sop up the media baby-sell don't usually ask such questions. Instead, taking their cue from the media, they applaud those who have babies while enjoying a revival of the old national pastime of pressuring those who don't have them, labeling them as "selfish" should they choose not to follow the pack. They don't ask, Is it more selfish to have a child when there is a distinct possibility that his father may not live long enough to help raise him? Nor do those who apply pressure to others to have children generally consider that babies are *people* and not just the latest fad, the most recent of which may have been designer jeans—now, please note, out of fashion.

While during the early and mid-seventies there existed a rather refreshing trend to grant other people the right to decide whether or not they would have children, there is now so little cultural support for this idea that in August of 1982 the National Association for Optional Parenthood folded. The whole concept of freedom of choice, even among many who espouse it, has slid backward and currently has a new definition: The "liberal" message now being broadcast is that it's all right to decide to *wait* to have children, and even all right to terminate a pregnancy if the timing is wrong. But it is not all right to decide not to have a child. The T-shirt was right—we haven't come a long way. We still bow to conformity.

When I listen to young women who are wrestling with the decision as to whether to have a child, I feel as if I'm caught in a time warp. They are hearing the same old tired lines I heard twenty years ago: "You don't know what you're missing." "You'll never be a real woman until you have a child." "You're depriving your husband of the joys of fatherhood." "When are you going to start your family?" "Have you had tests?" "Have you thought about adoption?" "You're not getting any younger, you know." "Won't you regret it later if you wait too long and *can't* have children because you'll be too old?"

Because this last question may be one of the most important of the pressure-bearing questions that is asked, it must be challenged with another question: Which is worse? To regret *not* having a child, or to regret having one at some point down the road of his or her life? So many myths prevent this kind of thinking. No one ever tells the uninitiated that children are individual human beings and that no one knows in advance what sort of children they'll have. Instead we have the myth that if you do everything right (whatever that is) your child will turn out to be exemplary. The fact is that while good parenting may tip the odds in that direction, no matter what you do, many other factors affect the growth and development of the child: Beyond the parents and the child's individual personality, there are the schools, the neighborhood, the church, life's variables, and the peer group. And babies have a way of turning into terrible twos, sassy nines, snotty twelves, and crazy adolescents—and then the peer group may be one outside force that can influence a child more than anything else.

Nobody ever tells prospective parents these things. Parents who blithely assume that a sweet little baby will, of course, turn into an obedient and charming child may be setting themselves up for the most profound disappointment and heartbreak they will ever know. Naturally it could all turn out well. But should your child, for example, despite all you may do for him or her, become an incorrigible drug- or alcohol-abusing teenager who steals your possessions and money to buy the substance that makes him or her behave like a lunatic, if you are a caring parent, chances are you will spend thousands of your hours and thousands of your dollars on psychiatrists trying to find out why this person you used to know has become a vile stranger. And if you hang in there and see it all the way through, you will be thanked for your pain and loving devotion by a society that will hold *you* responsible for everything that went wrong.

Casualties

Tragic consequences can result when people have children as a result of social pressure or while under the influence of unrealistic expectations. When everything does not work out, they may regret it so much that they want to put them back where they came from. But of course they cannot do that, so what do they do?

They toss them out.

Becky is just *one* whose story speaks to this sort of parental regret. She is the sixteen-year-old daughter of a college professor and his traditional wife. In high school she went wild: she smoked cigarettes, wouldn't come home when she was supposed to or came home drunk, smoked pot, and verbally abused her parents. She was, her parents said, "ruining our lives." In their life plans this daughter was supposed to *enhance* their lives, because that's what the hype of the day led them to believe. Having failed badly at that role, she was no longer welcome in the home. She now lives on the street in beautiful downtown Palo Alto with her roommate, Cindy, who is also sixteen. "Phone-booth mate" is probably a more accurate term, for if you wish to reach either of the girls, you call the number of "their" phone booth on the corner.

Or there is Janie, the daughter of two people who purchased the dream and had two children. The well-educated parents were rather perfect. Unfortunately Janie was imperfect—neither beautiful nor accomplished, and an utter disappointment to her mother, who fell into the habit of drumming it into her child's head that she was ugly, that no boy would ever like her, that she would never amount to anything. Janie's mother beat her, and once cut her hair so short that the child looked bald. This disappointed mother walked out on her when Janie was just thirteen, leaving her in the care of a father who had other things on his mind. Janie is sixteen now. She writes sad poems and sings sad songs, hungers for love, and will sleep with just about any young man who approaches her. She sees their desire to use her sexually as evidence that she's attractive, that her mother was wrong. She told me, "My mother said I'd never get guys. Well, I've got *lots* of guys. I'll show her."

There is twenty-two-year-old Evan, who runs around with teen-agers because, as he explained to me, "My parents never let me be a real child. I had to be a perfect gentleman and a perfect student so they'd look good to their friends. I couldn't listen to rock because it was 'pornographic.' I had an ulcer by the time I was fourteen. I'm just trying to go through a stage of development I missed." As I write these words I am still recovering from the trauma of Evan's recently having tried to commit suicide.

They come and they go, these poor lost kids. Some of them stay at our house for a while because they have nowhere else to live, and we haven't the heart to put the more innocent ones out on the street. And while few actually live here, most nights we sit down to a dinner table of anywhere from six to ten people, and we are a family of four. And when we do sit down, I know that some of the kids who join us aren't remotely missed at their own tables, even though they are still living at home. They are burdens, superfluous in the very places where they ought to be loved and where at least one parent should let them know they are special.

"Good people" are shocked when their middle-class neighbors cannot cope and turn their backs on their own children. There is an assumption that it is rare for parents to be so indifferent, frustrated, disappointed, or angry at their children that they, in essence, desert them. But it isn't all that rare, and a fact that must be faced is that some people don't even *like* their own kids.

In an article, "Who Will Help the Children?" (1982), Dotson Rader tells more tragic stories and gives us the staggering dimensions of the problem. He writes about children, some as young as eleven, who live on the street and earn their keep through prostitution. He tells us that many of the children don't live very long—150,000 of them disappear each year—they die from untreated illness and brutality: The leading cause of death for young boys is rectal hemorrhaging from too much sodomy. More than *eighty percent of these children,* he says, *come from white middle- and upper-class families.* "Without exception," writes Rader, "those [children] I met seemed starved for adult affection and regard but were fearful, filled with resentment against parents who they believe never loved them.

Oddly enough, they blame themselves and wonder what is so bad about them that made their parents love them so little." Such children's perceptions of their parents' lack of feeling for them are corroborated by the fact that *the majority of runaways are never reported missing by their parents.*

I must repeat: eighty percent of these hundreds of thousands of children are from middle- and upper-class families. Of those who were "planned," one can only wonder *why* they were planned. Apparently the parents all wanted babies, but did any of them want *real* children and everything that goes along with having them? The existence of these children from "good" middle-class homes in which they are no longer welcome causes me to fear that right now—right this minute—more of these "good" people are planning to have children, people who absolutely do not have what it takes for the long haul. Swayed by the media and cultural pressures, they not only don't realize what an awesome undertaking raising children is, but have no real concept that having a child is a life-long commitment.

The Penalties of Population Growth

Although parents who desert their children cannot be excused, the blame belongs to a society that extols only the mythical joys and none of the responsibilities or potential dark sides of the parental role, a society that is mostly nonsupportive of people once it has turned them into parents, and a society that perpetually encourages people to have children without giving the matter thought. Fundamentalist coercion in this area is but an exaggerated version of American cultural mores; both have a materialistic agenda and show no genuine concern for real living children.

Ironically, had it not been for the media hype after World War II and the resultant baby boom, the chances are that not only would some of us not have had children, the children we did have probably would not have been as troublesome as some of them are. For, as Landon Jones points out in *Great Expectations* (1980), had it not been for the boom generation, the whole sixties drug scene associated with it would probably not have bloomed on college campuses and then filtered down to our high schools and our junior high schools. Also ironically, had it not been for the baby-boom generation that created a population explosion, probably many of today's parents would have an easier time coping with the stresses of raising children, especially through the teen years.

Many experts tell us that overpopulation is threatening our very life-support system, but few make a connection between overpopulation and how difficult the parental role has become, not just because of the legacy left to us by the sixties generation, but because our highly complex and impersonal culture has added many more jobs to the parental role. I suspect that this aspect of overpopulation has been long neglected, simply because most of the experts who deal with this issue are not mothers, so they are blissfully ignorant of how difficult rapid growth has made parenting.

Living where I do, I have experienced the detrimental effects of this sort of growth at a very personal level. Life here in the Santa Clara Valley—now popularly referred to as "Silicon Valley"—is complicated by high tech, but nothing has brought so many changes and complications as the *sheer numbers of people*. Not only have I been an eyewitness to the ravages that have been wreaked upon this once-serene agricultural mecca, but like other parents, I have been deeply affected by an absurd cost of living, the rise in crime rates (we are now Number 9 in the nation), and the erosion of our educational system—all caused by our rapid growth.

Contrasting what I do to what my mother did in serener, less populous times, I come up with a rather interesting list of chores that were not on my mother's regular agenda. For openers, as rapid growth had not yet turned the community into the highest cost-of-living area in the nation, my mother didn't have to work outside the home. Even ten years ago, none of the mothers I knew worked. Today nearly all do because they must.

Mothers today, because they must do many other things my mother never had to do, run around on treadmills. Where my mother never made an appearance at my high school until the day I graduated, I am constantly at the school because I must confer with everyone to ensure that my kids are getting something half as good as the education that came my way automatically. Of course, one reason why some married mothers work outside the home is so they can afford to send their kids to *small* (normal-size, in my day) private schools that they don't have to monitor perpetually.

It never occurred to my mother that one of her children might get hit by a car in a suburban neighborhood. We live on a tree-lined street in an old section of Palo Alto that looks deceptively like the neighborhood street of my childhood. Recently enough so that it still makes my stomach churn, one of my worst fears was realized: my son was hit by a speeding car. So I did another thing my mother never had to do: I called 911, and after they had rushed here and administered first-aid to keep him from bleeding to death, I then spent six hours in the emergency ward of Stanford Hospital while a medical team examined and X-rayed my child and a plastic surgeon stitched his arm back together. This was because a *commuter* had used a once-quiet residential street to avoid throughway traffic and stop lights. This is now a common practice, which has turned many once-safe streets into danger zones. Screeching brakes perpetually bring me to the window on the days that I'm home to make sure someone has not hit one of our cats or someone's child.

After my son got hit by a car, I reached for the telephone directory to register a complaint about commuters using our street to avoid traffic signals. The phone book I dragged off the shelf is now five inches thick as compared to the one I had ten years ago, which was only one inch thick. Just looking up the number was quite a chore, as the type size is now much smaller to allow for more listings. On finding what I thought was the appropriate one, I dialed the number and was transferred six times until I got a recording. I gave up.

While I found no comfort in being unable to register my complaint, after the accident we found "comfort" in realizing that we were by no means alone when well-wishing parents marveled that in all of our years living here, this was the first time one of our children had sustained such a serious injury. It seems that "simply everyone" has been hit by a car at one time or another. My mother had four kids. Nobody ever worried about such things then.

Recently I had to drive thirty miles to San Jose to take my son to court for a bicycle traffic citation. The offense was riding double in his own neighborhood. Prior to that we went to court because he was riding a friend's bike that wasn't registered, and prior to that I had to take him to register *his* bike. My mother, who had four kids who rode double and triple, had never heard of such a thing as a bike license, never *once* took anyone to traffic court. Procedures have changed because of numbers of people. Bike theft, unheard of twenty years ago in our area, is now commonplace. Not because all people are less moral, but because there are more people, hence more who aren't moral. So we must register our bikes and travel thirty miles to deal with minor infractions. But riding double is no longer a minor infraction, simply because the heavy traffic makes it unsafe to do so. It is, in fact, unsafe to ride a bike at all, and there is now a campaign on to get kids to wear crash helmets.

When I was growing up my mother never had to keep her children from running around on days when there were smog alerts. Virtually every kid I know, my own included, has pollution-related allergies, and quite a number of parents must not just keep the kids still on the bad days, but take them regularly to allergists. My mother never knew what an allergist was. Nor did she have to make trips to the drug store to pick up the medications for allergies, or, as I did for a time, keep my child's room dust-free.

Another thing parents of my generation have had to do that my mother didn't even think about is find recreation for our kids. Inflation has knocked out movies, bowling, and other things that were popular when I was a kid. And sports, because the sheer numbers of people mean that there is very heavy competition, are now activities for the accomplished few. There are few places where teenagers can go just to be together and talk and listen to music. The creamery of the Fonz doesn't exist—kids are no longer welcome in such places because there are too many of them. People do not like teenagers because they are troublesome, and they are troublesome any time there are too many of them in one environment. And we wonder why electronic games are so popular.

Among the many things my mother never had to do is stand in long lines at the Department of Motor Vehicles—and practically everywhere else—or sit in a car in a gas line, which I have done, and which, according to the Electric Power Research Institute, I can anticipate doing again regularly, for in the next couple of years the truth of resource depletion will *really* hit.

Which brings to mind another thing my mother never had to do— drive her daughters everywhere for a two-year period and then for another one-year period because there were rapists on the loose. My mother never even had to lock her front door, but in addition to having to drive girls around because rapists were loose, during these periods we all were very cautious when *answering* our doors, even in broad daylight. We still are.

Before she died, however, my mother did know one of the true joys of population growth—that of having been reduced to a number, something to which we've all grown accustomed. As Philip Zimbardo has remarked, we aren't fully aware of how damaging it is to our spirit to have to produce two pieces of identification to verify our existence.

A Better World for Children

At every level we are experiencing the pains of growth, and one of the main reasons is that too many people who bought the feminine mystique lock, stock, and barrel had too many children. In the face of the current baby-sell and its possible consequences, one thing about motherhood needs to be re-emphasized. Given how very difficult our jobs have become and the fact that so many of us must now work, it is absolutely vital that our culture stop trivializing the role and start paying serious attention to it so mothers can get the help they need. As long as it is believed that being a mother is fun and easy, not only will women continue to buy that idea and be surprised when it isn't, but males will have no reason to pitch in and shoulder a fair part of the load.

I thought about this one day while I was watching a young father about thirty years old. I had taken my son to the hospital for a test, and both the young father and I were sitting in the waiting room—I while my son was being tested, and he while his wife was having a checkup. He had with him a little boy who looked to be about three years old and a small baby. Seeing him watch his children while his wife was being examined brought to mind the contrast between this man's experience and my own some eighteen years ago, when a man wouldn't be caught dead accompanying his wife to the doctor—unless, of course, she was dying and couldn't drive the car.

In any event, the father was holding the boy on his lap and the little boy in turn was holding the baby on *his* lap, feeding him his bottle, while the father had his arms gently wrapped around both of them. He answered the three-year-old's questions and talked to the baby too. At one point the father lifted everybody off his lap, kissed the three-year-old, dug in the diaper bag and pulled out a little book for him to look at, pulled out a diaper and powder, and then changed the baby with as much expertise as I ever possessed—a clear indication that it was something he did quite often.

As I watched it occurred to me that this was a father who really had children, as opposed to traditional males whose wives have them. These children quite probably were blessed with *two* parents. And as I sat there I felt a pang of envy and regret—for myself, for my children, and for my own husband, whose conversion from traditionalism to more genuine fatherhood had come much later. And I thought, That's how it should be from the very beginning. While certainly we are seeing more of this sort of loving fatherhood, we are not seeing enough of it. It is just this sort of involvement with the family, this sharing of the parental role, that I believe could make marriages richer and stronger and provide children with a real sense of family as they grow. Jessie Bernard concluded her exhaustive study of motherhood (*The Future of Motherhood,* 1974) with the words, "We cannot . . . afford to deprive either sex of the strengths of the other. Motherhood . . . is too important to leave to women. Inside or outside the home." Bernard calls for "a new balance" to preserve marriage and the family.

For millennia women have been told that the hand that rocks the cradle rules the world. If we use the power we truly have, if we begin to think in a more future-directed way when we plan our families, not only will our families be healthier, but the world will be a healthier place for them and for future generations.

Most rational people now agree that there is a connection between overpopulation, pollution, and resource depletion. Many experts can relate virtually every social ill we are now trying to cope with to overpopulation in the United States. Among them is Stanford biologist Professor Paul R. Ehrlich, who, in dozens and dozens of papers, articles, and books—*The Population Bomb; Population, Resources, Environment;* and *The End of Affluence*—provides hard, well-researched, and thoroughly documented facts, figures, and frightening predictions for the future if population growth continues at its present rate. Garrett Hardin of the University of Santa Barbara has for years warned of the consequences we are now seeing—15,000 new pollutants in the environment in one year, for example; the melting of the polar ice caps, an epidemic of cancer.

Ehrlich and Hardin and numerous other authorities, including biologists, sociologists, demographers, and even psychologists, leave no doubt in one's mind that overpopulation is a major underlying cause of famine, disease, air pollution, water pollution, inflation, war, shortages, violent crime, mental illness, alienation, and child abuse.

Should the combined efforts of the media baby-sell and the Religious New Right cause our population to grow at an even greater rate than it is growing now, with people being both pressured and coerced into having children they may be ill-prepared to take care of, we will lose far more than our rights. And before the pendulum could swing back in a balancing direction, all reverence for life would genuinely be lost, simply because the multitudes of people would cheapen the value of life. Not only would women be worn and burned-out before their middle years by being coerced into having too many children, but babies, truly made cheaper because of their dozens, would be tossed on the scrap heap. Life here could be as it is in India—hardly anyone in the world even cares if ten or twenty thousand Indian citizens are wiped out by disease.

Should it ultimately come to pass that freedom of choice and good sense are overwhelmed, and that overpopulation leads to ecological and social disaster, it would be folly to assume that there would not be a backlash. Right now there are those who believe that mandatory birth control should be the law of the land. Right now most of them are quiet because such is an unpopular view. One who has gone public with his ideas is Professor Edgar Chasteen, whose arguments in *The Case for Compulsory Birth Control* were persuasive enough to have evoked this comment from Ashley Montagu:

> I concur with your view and your conviction of urgency. The fact is that unless mankind solves its population problem it will be able to solve no other problem, and the catastrophe of the worst kind will result.

The book and Montagu's comment were published in 1971, when there were ten million fewer of us in the United States. How will these ideas be met when there are, say, twice as many of us? How unpopular will they be when it becomes general knowledge that too many people are making life intolerable for the whole species?

In the event that the pendulum should swing all the way to the right and the results are as disastrous as predicted, causing it to swing in the other direction, an ultimate irony might ensue. Those who would be born as a result of compulsory pregnancy laws would probably, as adults, be prohibited from reproducing. Precedent for legislating reproduction will have been set. In other words, if we can be forced to have children we don't want, we, as a people, can be deprived of the right to have the children we may want at some future date.

And it is the irresponsibility of the New Right agenda that could lead us to such an oppressive place. There, we would be left not just with environmental deterioration but with the multiplication of such problems as parental burnout, teenage rebellion, and child abuse. One need look no further than Utah for a future scenario of the net result of the damage when the cultural glorification of motherhood combined with the New Right agenda is realized. The Mormon image of motherhood could have come straight out of a TV commercial: perfect, happy children kept perfectly clean and well-behaved by perfect mothers fulfilled by their role. The ideal setup for unrealistic expectations and certain failure in the role.

While there are no pat formulas for family happiness and health, what we learn from the Utah example is this: All potential parents should have complete information on what caring for a child and raising one to adulthood is really like; no woman should be forced to have a child she doesn't want or for whom she cannot provide financially; those considering parenthood should honestly examine their own skills as potential parents, taking into account any unresolved conflicts they may have that could negatively affect the way in which they would care for children. Finally, because finances and marital stress go hand in glove, and both lead to parental stress, a question that I believe must be asked is "Can this marriage sustain the very real pressures of parenthood, and can we afford the high cost of bringing up baby?"

For those of us who want to see a better world for children, there is also a global question: Considering the impact of each new human being on the planet in terms of resources and pollution, how many, if any, children ought we each bring into the world today? Thinking globally isn't just an exercise in altruism but is also a way of thinking in terms of individual children and their welfare, because the next question that naturally follows is, "Is this the sort of world we want to bring children into?"

Because I have written candidly about the dark sides of parenthood, I have been frequently asked a different question: "If you had it to do over again, would you have children?" At this moment the question is a pertinent one, and I will answer it to illustrate how unthinking it is and how it leads to a more important question.

If I knew then what I know now, it ought to be obvious to anyone who thinks about it, not only would I know what all the dark sides of motherhood are, but, having stuck it out, I would have years of training in the parental role. That being the case, *were the year 1965* (when my first child was born), despite all of the bumps I most emphatically would repeat the performance. My husband and I are among the lucky ones, because along the way we changed and grew and became genuine parents who remain committed to our children for life. It is a commitment that requires great tenacity, personal sacrifice, and lots of unconditional loving, and some people burn out and can't make it.

We've made it. But even as family-centered as we have become over the years, *were the year 1982,* the question of having children would be a different matter. There is no doubt in my mind that we have, through much pain, developed what it takes to be loving and conscientious parents. There is every doubt in my mind, however, that we could afford the enterprise. There is even more doubt that the world we now live in is one in which we would want to bring as babies the children we love more with every passing year. And when I look into the future—say, twenty years beyond when those babies would reach adulthood—the doubt becomes a deeper one, as I see the mindless "pregnancy chic" and the Fundamentalist folly threatening to accelerate the deterioration of the quality of life on earth.

My vision of the future is grim, I know. And it begs a question: "Is it *possible* to make this a good world for living children and the children of the future?"

It is possible. The answer is within the grasp of our feminine hands. Women still have it within their power to alter the disastrous course we are on. We have it within our power to influence the course of history if we do just three things: first, think about the seriousness of having children; about how many we can actually manage and what their impact on the world will be; think about the issues that concern us—the threat to our power to determine how many times we will reproduce ourselves. Next, to preserve that power, begin by letting our national leaders know that we will not hold still and become pawns in the New Right's effort to seize control of our nation or enhance corporate profits by depriving us of our *basic* rights. And finally we must exercise the one right that is our greatest weapon—the right to vote.

It sounds so simple, but it is *our* vote that can tip the balance. Not only does our right to self-determination in the immediate future rest in our hands, but so does the future of democracy. Those hands that historically have rocked the cradle may turn out to be those that steady the world.

BIBLIOGRAPHY

Adams, June. "I Liked It Better When It Was Him Tarzan, Me Jane." *McCall's Working Mother,* November 1981.

Asbury, Herbert. *The Great Illusion: An Informal History of Prohibition.* New York: Doubleday & Company, 1950.

Arrington, Christine Rigby. "Thou Shalt Not Work." *McCall's Working Mother,* January 1982.

Bernard, Jessie. *The Future of Marriage.* New York: World Publishing Co., 1972; Bantam Books, 1973.

————. *The Future of Motherhood.* New York: Dial Press, 1974; Viking Penguin Inc., 1975.

Braden, Tom. "Anti-Abortion Morality is Meaningless to the Father of a Rape Victim." *San Jose Mercury News,* July 5, 1981.

Brownmiller, Susan. *Against Our Will.* New York: Simon & Schuster, 1975; Bantam Books, 1976.

Bush, Larry, and Richard Goldstein. "America's Moral Battleground." *San Francisco Chronicle,* "This World," July 5, 1981.

Caldicott, Helen. "This Beautiful Planet." *Speak Out Against the New Right,* Herbert F. Vetter, ed. Boston: Beacon Press, 1982.

Cass, Peg, ed. *Watch on the Right.* Vol. II, No. 3, March, 1982.

"Catholic Fraternity Praised: Reagan Backs School Prayer, Tougher Abortion Rules." Associated Press, August 3, 1982.

"The Changing Role of Women in the 80's." *The Peninsula Times Tribune,* February 18, 1981.

Chasteen, Edgar R. *The Case for Compulsory Birth Control.* Englewood Cliffs, New Jersey: Prentice-Hall, 1971.

"A Clash Over Worker Sex Harassment." Associated Press, April 22, 1981.

Clymer, Adam. "Women's Votes Are a Reagan Woe." *The New York Times,* November 19, 1981.

Conway, Flo, and Jim Siegelman. *Holy Terror: The Fundamentalist War on America's Freedoms in Religion, Politics, and Our Private Lives.* New York: Doubleday & Company, 1982.

Cooper, John Charles. *The Religious Pied Pipers.* Valley Forge, Pa.: Judson Press, 1980.

"Court Says Schmitz Has 2 Illegitimate Kids." *San Francisco Chronicle,* July 21, 1982.

Crawford, Alan. *Thunder on the Right: The "New Right" and the Politics of Resentment.* New York: Pantheon Books, 1980.

Crawford, Christina. "Conspiracy of Silence." *Ladies' Home Journal,* November 1981.

————. *Mommie Dearest.* New York: William Morrow, 1978; Berkeley, 1981.

"Crime's Link to Hard Times." Associated Press, August 9, 1982.

Danforth, Kenneth C. "The Cult of Mormonism." *Harper's,* May 1980.

Davis, Peter. *Hometown.* New York: Simon & Schuster, 1982.

DeCourcy, Peter and Judith. *A Silent Tragedy: Child Abuse in the Community.* New York: Alfred Publishers, 1973.

Disend, Michael. "Have You Whipped Your Child Today." *Penthouse,* February 1982.

Ehrlich, Paul R. *The Population Bomb.* New York: Sierra Club/Ballantine Books, 1968.

————. *Population, Resources, Environment.* Los Altos, California: William F. Kaufmann Co., 1970.

Eisler, Raine. "The Human Life Amendment and the Future of Human Life." *The Humanist,* September–October 1981.

Epps, Garrett. "Apostle of Abortion." *Science '82,* 1982.

"Equal Property Settlements in Divorce Called Unfair." *San Francisco Chronicle,* June 2, 1982.

"ERA Leaders Going After New Targets." *San Francisco Chronicle,* March 25, 1982.

Fager, Chuck. "Falwell and Co.–On the Skids . . . Or Speeding Up?" *In These Times, San Francisco Chronicle,* May 5–11, 1982.

Falwell, Jerry. *Listen America!* New York: Doubleday, 1980; Bantam, 1981.

Fishman, Walda Katz, and Georgia E. Fuller. "Unraveling the Right-Wing Opposition to Women's Equality." A special report published by Interchange Resource Center, 1981.

Follis, Ann Bowen. *I'm Not a Women's Libber, But . . .* New York: Avon, 1982.

Fontana, Vincent. *Somewhere a Child Is Crying.* New York: Macmillan, 1973.

Forster, Arnold, and Benjamin R. Epstein. *Danger on the Right.* New York: Random House, 1976.

Friedan, Betty. *The Feminine Mystique.* New York: W.W. Norton, 1963; Dell, 1977.

————. "Feminism's Next Step." *The New York Times Magazine,* July 5, 1981.

Galbraith, John Kenneth. "Economics of the Arms Race." *The Boston Review,* August 1982.

Gallup, George. "Poll on Women and Job Bias." *Los Angeles Times Syndicate,* 1982.

————. "Women Want Kids, Jobs Too, Poll Finds." *San Francisco Chronicle,* August 9, 1982.

George, Alice. *The Independent,* October 11, 1915.

Gill, David. *Violence Against Children.* Cambridge: Harvard University Press, 1971.

Gordon, Linda. "The Struggle for Reproductive Freedom," *Capitalist Patriarchy and the Case for Socialist Feminism,* Eisenstein, ed., New York: Monthly Review Press, 1978.

Greider, William. "Women vs. Reagan." *Rolling Stone,* August 19, 1982.

"The Growing Battle Over Would-Be Book Censors." *San Francisco Chronicle,* September 8, 1982.

"Growing Impact of Women in U.S. Labor Force." Associated Press, August 16, 1982.

Hadden, Jeffrey K., and Charles E. Swann, *Prime Time Preachers: The Rising Power of Televangelism.* Reading, Mass.: Addison-Wesley Publishing Co., 1981.

Harris, Mervin. "'Growing Conservatism' Not in Family Patterns." *Los Angeles Times,* December 23, 1981.

Harrison, Barbara Grizzuti. "The Woman Who Is Fighting the Law That Most Women Want." *McCall's,* April 1982.

Helfer, Ray E., and C. Henry Kempe. *The Battered Child,* third rev. ed. Chicago: University of Chicago Press, 1980.

Interchange, Vol. IV, No. 1, January, February, 1982.

Janeway, Elizabeth. *Man's World Woman's Place.* New York: William Morrow & Company, 1971; Dell, 1972.

————. "Incest: A Rational Look at the Oldest Taboo." *Ms.,* November, 1981.

Johnson, Sonia. *From Housewife to Heretic.* New York: Doubleday & Co., 1981.

Jones, Landon Y. *Great Expectations: America and the Baby Boom Generation.* New York: Coward, McCann & Geoghegan, 1980; Ballantine Books, 1981.

Kenyon, Karen. "A Pink Collar Worker's Blues." *Newsweek* (My Turn), October 4, 1982.

Komisar, Lucy. *The New Feminism.* New York: Franklin Watts, 1972.

LaHaye, Tim. *The Battle for the Mind: A Subtle Warfare.* Old Tappan, N.J.: Fleming H. Revell Co., 1980.

Langer, Walter C. *The Mind of Adolf Hitler.* New York: Basic Books, 1972; New American Library, 1978.

Lindner, Robert. *Must You Conform?* New York: Holt, Rinehart and Winston, 1956; Black Cat Grove Press, 1961.

McLaughlin, Loretta. "Behind the World Population Crisis." *Los Angeles Times,* June 30, 1982.

Montagu, Ashley. *The Natural Superiority of Women.* New York: Macmillan, 1952; Collier Books, 1968.

"Mormons Seek to Tackle Child-Abuse Problem." Associated Press, June 27, 1982.

"A Mother Too Young to Have Housing." *San Francisco Chronicle,* October 23, 1981.

Park, Charles. "Preachers, Politics, and Public Education: A Review of Right Wing Pressures Against Public Schooling in America." *Phi Delta Kappan,* May 1980.

Pierard, Richard V. *Bibliography of the New Christian Right.* Terre Haute, Indiana: Indiana State University, 1981.

Potts, Malcolm. "The Uncertain Journey." *Science '82,* March 1982.

Prescott, J. W. "Abortion and the 'Right to Life': Facts, Fallacies, and Fraud." *The Humanist,* July–August and November–December 1978.

Rader, Dotson. "Who Will Help the Children?" *Parade,* September 5, 1982.

"Reagan Adds Support to Anti-Abortion Fight." *San Francisco Chronicle,* September 9, 1982.

"Reagan Plan for Prayer in the Public Schools." *San Francisco Chronicle,* May 7, 1982.

Redekop, John H. *The American Far Right: A Case Study of Billy James Hargis and the Christian Crusade.* Grand Rapids, Mich.: William B. Erdmans Publishing Co., 1968.

Reed, J. D., and reported by Barbara Dolan/New York and Allessandra Stanley/Los Angeles. "The New Baby Bloom." *Time,* February 22, 1982.

"Report on Senator Schmitz's Son." *The Peninsula Times Tribune,* July 20, 1982.

Rivers, Caryl. "Teen Pregnancies Involve More Than Sex." *Los Angeles Times,* December 15, 1981.

————, and Rosalind Barnett. *Beyond Sugar and Spice*. New York: Ballantine Books, 1981.

Robertson, Ian. *Sociology*. New York: Worth Publishers Co., 1977.

Rubin, Nancy. "Women vs. Women." *Ladies' Home Journal,* March, 1982.

Rush, Florence. *The Best Kept Secret: Sexual Abuse of Children*. New York: McGraw-Hill, 1980.

Salter, Stephanie. "Teacher Burnout." *San Francisco Examiner,* July 12, 1982.

Sanger, Margaret. *Margaret Sanger: An Autobiography*. New York: W.W. Norton & Co., 1938; Dover, 1971.

"Schlafly Explains Failure of the ERA." *The Peninsula Times Tribune,* June 18, 1982.

"Schmitz Called Doting Father." *San Francisco Chronicle,* Associated Press, July 23, 1982.

"Schmitz's Lover Faces Child-Neglect Charge." *San Francisco Chronicle,* Associated Press, July 28, 1982.

Seawell, Mary Ann. "Segregation by Sex Remains the Mode at Most Workplaces." *The Peninsula Times Tribune,* August 27, 1982.

Sibert, Mimi H. Work quoted in *San Francisco Chronicle,* June 7, 1982.

Snyder, Craig W. "Censorship in America: Power Swings to Oppression." *Impact '82,* Number 4, published by the Institute for Family Research and Education, 1982.

Steinem, Gloria. "The Nazi Connection." *Speak Out Against the New Right,* Herbert F. Vetter, ed. Boston: Beacon Press, 1982.

"The Supreme Court's Rights." *San Francisco Chronicle,* September 9, 1982.

Sweeney, Joan. "Marriages that Last—Two Kinds." *San Francisco Chronicle Sunday Punch,* June 27, 1982.

Tanner, Leslie B., ed. *Voices From Women's Liberation*. New York: Signet Books, 1970.

Vetter, Herbert F., ed. *Speak Out Against the New Right*. Boston: Beacon Press, 1982.

"Watt Pays Brown a Compliment the Governor Rejects." *San Francisco Examiner,* September 9, 1982.

"A Way to God: Shock the Hell Out of the Kid." *San Francisco Examiner,* July 10, 1981.

Winokur, Scott. "The Tragedy of Abandoned Babies." *San Francisco Sunday Examiner & Chronicle,* May 28, 1982.

Wohl, Lisa Cronin. "The Sweetheart of the Silent Majority." *Ms.,* March 1974.

Yankelovich, Daniel. "Stepchildren of the Moral Majority." *Psychology Today,* November 1981.

Young, Perry Deane. *God's Bullies: Power Politics and Religious Tyranny.* New York: Holt, Rinehart and Winston, 1982.

INDEX

A

Abdnor, James, 154
Abel, Dr. Gene G., 74
Adams, June, 168
Adler, Jerry, 42
Adventures of Huckleberry Finn, The (Twain), 144
Against Our Will (Brownmiller), 49–50, 76
Aid to Families with Dependent Children, 70
Alan Guttmacher Institute, 123, 125
All in the Family (TV series), 60
Allen, Mary Kay, 67, 82
Allen-Bradley Corporation, 62
America First Committee, 151, 152
American Committee to Free Cuba, 116
American Far Right, The (Redekop), 57
American Humane Association, 98
American Humanist Association, 137
American Library Association, 144, 145
American Life Lobby, 32, 68
American Psychological Association, 16
Americans for Law and Order, 116
Amway Corporation, 62
Andress, Ursula, 60
Armstrong, Bishop James, 148
Armstrong, William, 154
Arrington, Christine Rigby, 7
Asbury, Herbert, 159
Assemblies of God, 157
Associated Press, 77, 80, 135
Authors' Guild, 144

B

Barnett, Juanita, 117, 120
Barnett, Rosalind, 128
Barney Miller (TV series), 60
Barnum, P. T., 65
Baron, James T., 11–12
Baruch, Grace, 128
Battle for the Mind, The (LaHaye), 137, 152
Baxter, Cathy, 70

Bayh, Birch, 32, 109
Bebb, Jane, 80
Bell, Dr., 98
Bem, Daryl, 2
Bem, Sandra, 2
Benson, Ezra Taft, 4, 8
Berk, Richard, 17
Bernard, Jessie, 28, 178
Best Kept Secret, The (Rush), 75, 97
Best Short Stories by Negro Writers, 144
Better Homes and Gardens, 145
Beyond Sugar and Spice (Rivers and Barnett), 128
Bielby, William T., 11
Billings, Robert, 156–57
Blackwell, Alice Stone, 91
Blackwell, Morton C., 157
Boone, Pat, 158
Boston Globe, The, 118
Braden, Tom, 33, 34
Bradley, Harry, 62
Brave New World (Huxley), 144
Briggs, Raymond, 144
Brown, Jerry, 165
Brownmiller, Susan, 49–50, 76
Buckley, William F., 115

C
Caldicott, Dr. Helen, 131
Cardinal Mindszenty Foundation, 116
Carey, John, 42
Case for Compulsory Birth Control, The (Chasteen), 179
Catcher in the Rye, The (Salinger), 144

Chasteen, Edgar, 179
Chevron, 157
Chicago Tribune, 24
Child Abuse Council, 70
Chisholm, Shirley, 40
Christian Broadcast Network, 4, 158
Christian Family Renewal, 138
Christian Freedom Federation, 62
Church, Frank, 32
Church of the Latter-Day Saints. *See* Mormon Church
Citizens for Biblical Morality, 49
Clayburgh, Jill, 60
Cleaver, Eldridge, 144
Committee for the Survival of a Free Congress, 62, 155
Comstock, Anthony, 48
Conference on Public Schools and the First Amendment, 109, 121, 136, 141, 148
Conservative Caucus, 49, 155
Conway, Flo, 112, 151, 152, 154
Coors, Joseph, 61, 62, 157
Corman, Avery, 145
Council of Twelve, 4
Council on Mind Abuse (COMA), 112
Crane, Philip, 154
Cranston, Alan, 161
Crawford, Alan, 66, 117, 120

D
Danforth, Kenneth C., 113
Danger on the Right (Forster and Epstein), 62, 151

Davis, Peter, 126–27

Delancey Street Foundation, 75

Denton, Jeremiah, 154

DeVos, Richard, 62

Diana (Princess of Wales), 60

Disend, Michael, 76, 138

Dixon, Greg, 77, 89, 121, 137, 138, 139, 145, 146, 148–49, 150

Dr. Ross Dog and Cat Food Company, 62

Dodds, Terry, 110–11, 137

Dolan, John "Terry," 165–66

Domestic Violence Prevention Act, 71

Dorman, Robert, 154

Dow Chemical Corporation, 62

Dunaway, Faye, 60

E

Eagle Forum, 4, 91, 110–11

Eagle Trust Fund, 116

Eagles Are Flying, 116

Edwards, Mickey, 154

Egan, Janet, 110, 137

Egeland, Leona, 2

Ehrlich, Paul, 131, 178–79

Eisler, Raine, 44

Electric Power Research Institute, 176

Emerson, Thomas I., 115

End of Affluence, The (Ehrlich), 178

Engelmayer, Paul A., 66

Englander-Golden, Paula, 19

Epstein, Benjamin R., 62, 151

Equal Employment Act of 1972, 115

Equal Rights Amendment (ERA), 106, 108, 118, 119, 153, 162

Evangelical Women's Caucus (EWC), 105

Evans, Bergen, 164

Evans, Richard, 150

Eversharp, Inc., 62

Exxon, 157

F

Fager, Chuck, 65

Falk, Gale, 115

Falwell, Jerry, 1, 4, 6, 8, 26–27, 36, 40, 48, 50, 54, 57, 64, 66, 96, 104, 115, 124, 129–30, 139, 143, 149, 156, 158, 161, 165

Families Anonymous, 84

Family Circle, 145

"Family Home Evening," 113

Family Protection Act, 26, 36, 69, 71, 122, 124, 142, 144, 165

Father Christmas (Briggs), 144

Father-Daughter Incest (Herman and Hirschman), 74

Federation of Republican Women, 116

Feminine Mystique, The (Friedan), 22

Feminist Movement in Germany—1894–1933, The (Evans), 150

Firing Line (TV show), 115

Fishman, Walda Katz, 67

Flick-Reedy Corporation, 62

Follis, Ann, 104–5

Fontana, Dr. Vincent, 70, 72, 79

Forerunner, 71

Forster, Arnold, 62, 151

Freemen Institute, 161

Friedan, Betty, 22, 25, 28, 29, 126

From Housewife to Heretic (Johnson), 46

Fugate, Richard, 71

Fuller, Georgia, 67

Future of Marriage, The (Bernard), 28

Future of Motherhood, The (Bernard), 28, 178

Fyfe, James, 135

G

Gabler, Mel, 143–44

Gabler, Norma, 143–44

Garn, Jake, 154

George, Alice, 90, 91

Giaretto, Henry, 73

Gillogley, Gloria, 87–88

Glasser, Ronald, 144

Goebbels, Joseph Paul, 150

God's Bullies: Power Politics and Religious Tyranny (Young), 166

Goldwater, Barry, 155

Good Housekeeping, 145

Goodbye, I Love You (TV movie), 59

Goodman, Ellen, 118

Gordon, Dr. Sol, 124

Gramm, Phil, 154

Grapes of Wrath, The (Steinbeck), 144

Grassley, Charles, 154

Great Expectations (Jones), 58, 135, 173

Great Illusion, The (Asbury), 159

Gregory, Dick, 40

Greider, William, 160

Gulf Oil Company, 62

H

Hall, Dr., 98

Hardin, Garrett, 178–79

Harlem Hospital, 41

Harris, Paul, 66

Hatch, Orrin, 34, 36, 154, 161

Hatcher, Chris, 78

Hawkins, Paula, 154

Hayakawa, S. I., 162

Haynes, Susanne G., 24

Helms, Jesse, 32, 33, 34, 36, 48, 70, 139

Henry Regnery Company, 62

Heritage Foundation, 61–62, 155

Herman, Judith Lewis, 74

Hitler, Adolf, 55, 149–50, 151, 152

Holt, Rinehart and Winston, 110

Holy Terror (Conway and Siegelman), 112, 151, 153, 161–62

Home Insurance Company, 66

Homemakers Equal Rights Association (HERA), 104

Hometown (Davis), 127

"How to Keep the Cousin You Hate from Spending the Whole Weekend at Your

House and Maybe Longer," 110

Hughes, Langston, 144

Human Life Amendment, 34, 35

Human Life Bill, 34, 35, 48

Humanist, The, 44

Humanist Association, 153

Humble Oil Company, 62

Humphrey, Gordon, 154

Hunt's Foods, 62

Huxley, Aldous, 144

Hyde, Henry, 33, 36

I

Illich, Ivan, 19

I'm Not a Women's Libber, but . . . (Follis), 104

Impact, 124

Independent, The, 90

"Indifference of Women, The" (Blackwell), 91

Institute for Family Research and Education, 124

Interchange, 61

Intercollegiate Society for Individualists, 152

International Fertility Research Program, 42

J

Jepsen, Roger A., 122, 154

John Birch Society, 104, 116, 161

Johnson, Sonia, 46, 99, 102, 104, 106–9, 112

Jones, Jim, 158

Jones, Landon Y., 58, 86, 135, 140, 173

K

Kasten, Bob, 154

Kenmetal, Inc., 62

Kennedy, Edward M., 33

Kenyon, Karen, 15

Kimball, Spencer, 4

Kleiman, Carol, 24

Komisar, Lucy, 150

Koop, Dr. C. Everett, 156

Knott's Berry Farm, 62

Kramer vs. Kramer (Corman), 144

Krug, Judith P., 145

L

Ladies' Home Journal, 2, 91, 103, 145

LaHaye, Tim, 109, 112, 137, 138, 150, 152, 165

Langley Porter Psychiatric Institute, 78

Larson, Bob, 129

Laxalt, Paul, 154, 165

Lear, Norman, 60

Levitan, Sar A., 127

Lieberman, Alicia, 78

Life, 59

Lilly Endowment Foundation of Indianapolis, 152

Lindner, Dr. Robert, 163

Listen America! (Falwell), 1, 6, 50, 129

Little House in the Woods (Wilder), 144

Los Angeles Times, 127

Lou Grant (TV series), 60

Lowman, Louise, 37–38

Lugar, Richard, 145

M

Mademoiselle, 144

Magazine Publishers Association Conference, 145

Making It with Mademoiselle, 144

Manion, Clarence, 151

M*A*S*H (TV series), 60, 118

Maude (TV series), 60

McCabe, Charles, 40

McCall's, 145

McCall's Working Mother, 7, 17, 168

McCarthy, Sen. Joseph, 116

McCloskey, Paul N., 45

McClure, James, 154

McDonald, Larry, 154

McGovern, George, 32

McKelvy, Doris, 85

Mecklenburg, Marjory E., 156

Mein Kampf (Hitler), 150

Miller, Jeanne, 87

Milliken, Roger, 62

Montagu, Ashley, 99–102, 179

Moral Majority, Inc., 4, 26, 32, 33, 34, 35, 38, 46, 49, 58, 62, 65–66, 71, 77, 91, 145, 150, 155, 167

Mormon Church, 4, 32, 34, 66–67, 80–84, 104, 106–9, 113, 161

Morris, Desmond, 144

Motorola, 62

Moyer, Dr. Wayne, 142

Ms., 116

Must You Conform? (Lindner), 163

"My Turn" (*Newsweek* column), 15

N

Naked Ape, The (Morris), 144

National Association for Optional Parenthood, 169

National Association of Biology Teachers, 142

National Association of Manufacturers, 62

National Coalition of American Nuns, The, 69

National Conservative Political Action Committee, 155, 166

National Organization of Women (NOW), 115

National Right-to-Life Committee, 4, 32, 34, 55, 91, 155

National Right-to-Life News, 54

Natural Superiority of Women, The (Montagu), 99

"Nazi Connection" (Steinem), 150

"New Baby Bloom, The," 169

New Feminism, The (Komisar), 150

New Right Report, 157

New York Times, The, 85, 145, 153, 157

Newsweek, 15, 42, 145

Nickles, Don, 154

1984 (Orwell), 144

Norris, Dr. Murray, 138

O

Oakland Housing Authority, 38

O'Connor, Sandra Day, 157

Of Mice and Men (Steinbeck), 144

Office of Adolescent Pregnancy Programs, 156

Office of Intellectual Freedom of the American Library Association, 145

Old Time Gospel Hour, The (TV show), 4, 64, 65, 66, 96, 158

One Day at a Time (TV series), 60

Orwell, George, 144

Otto, Max, 148

Our Bodies, Ourselves, 46

P

Parents Anonymous, 73, 84

Parents of Minnesota, Inc., 110

Parents United, 73

Passages (Sheehy), 144, 145

Peninsula Times Tribune, The, 2, 11

Penthouse, 76, 138

People, 145

People for the American Way, 144, 145

Personality of a Child Molester, The (Bell and Hall), 98

Philadelphia Inquirer, 161

Phillips, Howard, 49

"Phyllis Schlafly Report, The," 116

Planned Parenthood, 39, 40, 65, 138

Poor Pay More, The (TV documentary), 63

Population, Resources, Environment (Ehrlich), 178

Population Bomb, The (Ehrlich), 178

Potts, Dr. Malcolm, 42–44

Powers, Carol, 59

Powers, Joe, 59

Pro-Family Action Committee, 91

Psychology Today, 123, 145

Q

Quayle, Dan, 154

R

Rader, Dotson, 172

Reagan, Ronald, 154, 156, 157–58

Redbook, 17, 145

Redekop, John H., 57

Republic Corporation, 62

Republican Party, 116

Rivers, Caryl, 127–28

Robertson, Pat, 4, 158

Rock (Larson), 129

Rolling Stone, 160

Rosenberg, Dr. Leon, 41

Rubin, Nancy, 2, 91, 94, 103

Rush, Florence, 75, 97, 98

S

Sakharov, Andrei, 152

Salinger, J. D., 144

Salter, Stephanie, 141

San Francisco Chronicle, 31, 37, 38, 40, 65, 74, 143, 167

San Francisco Examiner, 87

San Francisco Sunday Examiner & Chronicle, 56, 69

Sanger, Margaret, 40, 48

Schick Safety Razor Company, 62

Schlafly, Phyllis, 1, 4, 36, 91, 96, 104, 110, 115–20, 124, 151, 165

Schmidling, Donald L., 148

Schmitz, John, 164–65

Science, 44

Science '82, 44

Sears, Roebuck and Co., 62, 151

Seawell, Mary Ann, 11

Senate Committee on Labor and Public Welfare, 40

700 Club, The (TV talk show), 4, 158

Sexual Behavior Clinic, 74

Sheehy, Gail, 144, 145

Sibert, Dr. Mimi H., 75

SIECUS, 138

Siegelman, Jim, 112, 151, 152, 154

Skousan, W. Cleon, 161

Slaughterhouse-Five (Vonnegut), 144

Smith, Jaclyn, 60

Society for the Suppression of Vice, 48

Somewhere a Child Is Crying (Fontana), 70, 72

Soul on Ice (Cleaver), 144

Spacek, Sissy, 60

Spindale and Cherokee Mills, 62

Sports Illustrated, 145

Stein, Rabbi Jonathan, 148–49

Steinbeck, John, 144

Steinem, Gloria, 41, 150

Stephen, Beverly, 60

Stolley, Richard, 145

Stop ERA, 4, 32, 91, 108, 116

Stop Immorality on TV, 116

Summer, Donna, 60

Symms, Steven, 154

T

Technical Corporation of America, 62

Tedrow, Mary, 94, 96

Tell Me Where It Hurts (TV movie), 59

Terkel, Studs, 144

These Times, 65

"This Beautiful Planet" (Caldicott), 131

"This World" (*San Francisco Chronicle*), 37, 143, 167

Thomas, Carl, 145

"Thou Shalt Not Work" (Arrington), 7

365 Days (Glasser), 144

Thunder on the Right (Crawford), 66

Time, 58, 145, 169

Tormes, Yvonne, 98

Truman, Harry S, 159

Twain, Mark, 144

U

United Press International, 77

United Steel Corporation, 62

United Way, 65

"Unraveling the Right-Wing Opposition to Equality" (Fishman and Fuller), 67

U.S. News & World Report, 145

V

Van Buren, Abigail, 145

Viguerie, Richard A., 155, 157
Vogue, 60
Vonnegut, Kurt, 144

W
Wall Street Journal, The, 66
Wallop, Malcolm, 154
Warner, John, 154
Washington, George, 143
Washington Post, The, 31
Washington Post–ABC News
  Poll, 44
Watt, James, 157, 165
*Webster's New Collegiate Dic-
  tionary,* 144
Weyrich, Paul, 62, 155
*What's Happening to the
  American Family* (Levitan
  and Belous), 127
"Who Is Raising Our Children?"
  (Fugate), 71
"Who Will Help the Children?"
  (Rader), 172
Wilder, Laura Ingalls, 144

Wilson, Pete, 165
Winokur, Scott, 69, 70
Wohl, Lisa Cronin, 115
Woman's Day, 145
Women's Psychology Quarterly,
  19
Wood, Robert E., 62, 151
Working (Terkel), 144
Wyckoff, Dean, 167

Y
Yankelovich, Daniel, 123
Young, Betty, 111
Young, Perry Deane, 166
Young Americans for Freedom,
  116
"Your Child from One to Six,"
  145

Z
Zack, Brian G., 44
Zappert, Larraine T., 16–17
Zero Population Growth, 138
Zimbardo, Philip, 114, 158, 177

THE AUTHOR

Shirley Rogers Radl is the author of several books that have made readers think about their lives, including *Mother's Day Is Over* and *The New Mother's Survival Guide*. With Philip Zimbardo, she is also the author of *The Shy Child*. Shirley Rogers Radl has been a leader in the population control movement, a book reviewer, and a nine-to-five secretary. She currently runs Quality of Life, an organization that educates the public about the threats—social, political, and environmental—endangering the quality of our lives. Her articles have appeared in *Life, Cosmopolitan, Ladies' Home Journal,* and many other national magazines. She is the mother of two teenage children.